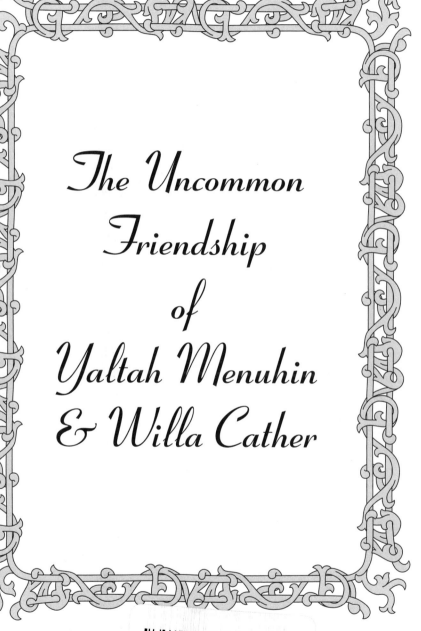

The Uncommon
Friendship
of
Yaltah Menuhin
& Willa Cather

The Uncommon Friendship of Yaltah Menuhin & Willa Cather

by

LIONEL ROLFE

This book is dedicated to
Boriana Vladeva
who made me believe in myself

And it was with the critical support of Boriana Vladeva, Nigey Lennon, Karen Kaye, Lorene Pike, Ronald Martinetti, Willa Woolston and John Ahouse it became a completed manuscript. The letters that Willa Cather wrote to my mother are now at Princeton University. Some of the photos were provided by Esther and Al Shak; the rest were in my mother's possession. I also have her diaries and notebooks.

American Legends Publishing
distributed by California Classics Books
www.americanlegends.com
ISBN: 1-879395-46-0

Preface

I very much enjoyed reading Lionel Rolfe's memoir of his mother, family and Willa Cather. Whereas conventional memoirs, biographies, and other stories of the artist focus upon the individual and her/his career, Rolfe's book is a multigenerational story of a family, and it's quite remarkable in this perspective, as well as from its being written by the third generation of that family.

I was particularly interested also in Willa Cather's relationship with the Menuhins, and especially with Rolfe's mother and grandmother, something I found sometimes contradictory (Cather's defense of Rolfe's grandmother, despite her hard treatment of his mother) and always moving.

I ended the book with deepened understanding of the special relationship between Rolfe's mother and Willa Cather, and appreciated it for that reason. But mainly I appreciated it because of insights it enabled about the family of the Menuhins, and about what it meant to be a third and female prodigy in that family.

It is a deeply humanizing reminder of actual people who create the art, and who create the conditions of artistic performance.

-- Sue Rosowski
University of Nebraska

Table of Contents

Willa Cather

Dear Yaltah:

This is a copy of the photograph which you and Hephzibah said you liked. We wish you a happy Christmas. Excuse my hurt hand, please.

An inscribed photo from Willa: "Dear Yaltah: This is a copy of the photograph which you and Hephzibah said you liked. We wish you a happy Christmas. Excuse my hurt hand, please."

Yaltah in Paris about the same time she met Willa Cather   Photo-Lipnitzki

LIPNITZKI
PARIS

Author's Introduction

In the largest sense, this book is about the relationships that women artists have with their families and their creativity.

In particular it is about a relationship that developed in the early 1930s between a middle-aged writer, Willa Cather, and a ten-year-old girl, my mother, the prodigy pianist Yaltah Menuhin. Yaltah was the youngest sister of violinist Yehudi Menuhin and pianist Hephzibah Menuhin. It was the opinion of important musical observers, right from the beginning, that she may have been the most musically talented of the three Menuhin children.

When Yaltah died, several obituaries cited her talent. As *The Guardian* put it, "Rudolf Serkin, who taught both sisters the piano, thought Yaltah the more talented. But, in temperament, she was less robust than Hephzibah, who fought more successfully against their parents' reluctance that either should have a musical career, and who was so close to Yehudi that Yaltah was made to feel an awkward third."

The obituaries noted that Yehudi had stated that Yaltah was the most talented of the three. He told me that as well, and I don't think he was saying it gratuitously. He kept repeating that Yaltah was not up to the rigors of touring. There was enough truth in his statement to accept it at face value. But I thought my mother's "fragility" was a bit overstated.

My mother found her stride in pursuing her music near the end of her life -- when her brother and husbands were no longer on the scene.

This tale will not be a story full of lurid details of a scandalous illicit romance, especially since speculation about Cather's sexual orientation has become virtually institutionalized among some academics. It is, however, the story of how an older woman provided a younger woman with a role model.

Willa was unique for her era. In the early 20th century, women were not welcome into the arts or the sciences or even the professions. Yet Cather attended the University of Nebraska, quickly became a leading newspaper writer and essayist, then editor of a famed national magazine, and finally the author of arguably some of the best American short stories and novels.

As a youngster, people sensed that Willa was destined to be something special. She had wanted to become a doctor, and not only worked as a doctor's assistant, but took to calling herself "Doctor" and wearing a man's suit. But she ended up as a writer when the local newspaper published an essay she had written. She was struck by the sight of her name in print -- and that, she later admitted, is why she pursued a writing career. Not surprisingly, most of her literary protagonists were strong women.

At one point the very young Willa Cather wrote for a newspaper because her father, a banker, repossessed one, and turned it over to his daughter.

Yaltah, on the other hand, was beaten down as a young girl, abused by her parents and even her brother and sister.

Willa, without directly urging Yaltah to rebel against her family, gave her the strength and backbone to become her own person.

Perhaps the most important lesson Cather taught Yaltah was to be her own woman, and her own artist. She provided the counterbalance to Yaltah's mother, Marutha, who only allowed Yaltah and her sister, Hephzibah, to study the piano because it was a good tool for attracting a husband.

Cather's second lesson was to teach Yaltah a sense of place, that sense which pervaded everything Willa wrote.

My mother, more so than others, required a safe haven. She had grown up in Northern California, and Europe -- Paris, Berlin, London. She then lived nearly two decades with my father in Los Angeles, a city she hated. She did not achieve some peace until she returned to spend the last four decades of her life in London.

All those years she wandered before coming to her final home in London were haunted by that need for a sense of place that Cather had instilled.

Willa's novels are always about that sense of place, from *My Antonia* to *O'Pioneers!* to *Death Comes for the Archbishop*. Place is everything in Willa's writings.

To Cather, people were products of the land. Cather saw Nebraska transformed from harsh plains to rich farmland. She showed how the men and women who conquered the land were molded by the process.

Yaltah learned that lesson by osmosis, by spending a lot of time with Cather and by reading and re-reading her books over different periods of her life -- always returning to the lessons Willa had to teach whenever she felt adrift.

When she felt the most "at sea" Yaltah would begin read-ing Willa's books, or if she really felt a need of being close to her, she would take them out and read them again. Even after Cather was long dead, Yaltah could turn to her mentor on the printed page.

CHAPTER ONE

Prologue: Letters from "Aunt Willa"

It must have been in the early 1950s in that paradoxical place of seacoast, desert sun, and brush fires that is Southern California. No fires were burning in the primeval canyons just then, and no great rains were falling. It was simply one of those glorious Southern California summer Sunday mornings when the sun was everywhere in my parents' bedroom.

Usually on a Sunday morning, they got their privacy. But sometimes the family assembled in the master bedroom because it admirably served as a family room as well. Part of their room was an entrance to another room that had only one small window and a low ceiling. At night we used that attic as a planetarium and imagined that the stars projected on the ceiling were real. Because the roof was low, in order to use the ceiling for the projector, you had to recline on large pillows on the wooden floor.

It was probably a mild morning, when summer veers into fall. It was not easy for the sun to shine through the windows, hung deep into the two-foot wide walls of the large two-story home where we lived in Long Beach, California.

It all felt very cozy. My parents, Benjamin and Yaltah, were lying in bed, and my brother Robby and I were nearby. My mother had brought out her shoe box full of letters from "Aunt Willa." She read one of the letters which described me as a baby, in most complimentary terms, and laughed at the memories. At other points she cried as she read.

Aunt Willa, she explained, was the mother her own mother Marutha had never been. If not openly, certainly in her heart of hearts, my mother thought of her mother as a witch.

As I watched her life unfold, it was plain to me that Yaltah Menuhin had good reason to feel the way she did. For the last decades of both their lives, mother and daughter had spoken only once, and that was after Yaltah's brother Yehudi had cajoled Marutha and Yaltah into a telephone call. After a valiant attempt, Yaltah hung up and never talked to her mother again.

My mother had been twenty when she married my father, then a young soldier in the Army who had gone AWOL to marry her. Amidst a storm of publicity, aided in part by Yaltah's father's open hostility to the marriage, the couple eloped. Moshe Menuhin was if nothing else direct about what he thought, abrasive as that often was. He hated the young lieutenant and told the newspapers he was "worse than Hitler."

Ben Rolfe was not famous, but the woman he married, a pianist, was -- because she was the sister of violinist Yehudi Menuhin, regarded as the greatest musical prodigy of the 20th century.

My mother had grown up without a real understanding of money, a characteristic she maintained even as she grew older and became much poorer.

Her early years as an army wife had left an emotional scar. When I was in my infancy, my crib was often the top drawer of an old bureau in Southern rooming houses and hotels.

Yaltah lived in dreary, cockroach infested places to be

Yaltah standing in front of our Long Beach house, below the room where she read me letters from Willa Cather

close to my father, who was stationed at Oak Ridge, Tennessee where work was proceeding on the atom bomb.

Confronted with the salt-of-the-earth about whom she had only read, Yaltah turned to writing long letters to Willa, and Willa wrote back.

That summer morning as my mother read the letters it seemed to me as if Cather had been amazingly romantic. She talked about how the pictures my mother had sent her showed I must have been the most beautiful baby in the world. She also advised my mother, who must have been contemplating divorce, to stay with my father even in the face of intense scorn from her parents.

CHAPTER TWO

A Life-Long Child

In October, 1941, Yaltah eloped with Ben to Reno and then followed him around from military camp to military camp for four years. Medford, Oregon, where I was born, was one of these.

After the war, my father settled with my mother in San Francisco. That was before my grandparents succeeded in driving them to Los Angeles.

From the beginning, Moshe made various proclamations about Ben, or "Bud," as he was known. At the point he met my mom he was just a soldier, a grunt, an attorney in private life. Moshe and Marutha felt he was not good enough for their daughter. Besides, they felt she was being ungrateful, for they were doing their best to find her a suitable mate.

"We hardly know the boy," Moshe said. "He has visited in our home several times along with other young fellows, but we didn't know which was which."

Moshe issued a statement a bit later, in case his meaning wasn't clear:

"Our three children, Yehudi, Hephzibah and Yaltah, exactly like their mother, are innocent and impractical idealists.

"They are great givers, spiritually as well as materially. All through their life, takers will take advantage of their infinite kindness and sweetness.

"In the case of Bud, all we pray and hope now is that he, after having met Yaltah only two or three times, will prove himself worthy of her."

They issued several more statements and made various quips indicating it was unlikely Ben would ever be able to prove himself worthy, no matter if he were he a combination of Albert Einstein and Jesus Christ.

Take this gem: "I wish to correct an impression that this marriage has our blessing or that I will aid this young man to finance a honeymoon if his soldier pay is not enough.

"He is my daughter's husband, but he is not my son-in-law. He must win our respect and affection, and so far, he is far, far from it … He must obtain our forgiveness for this absurd undertaking."

I was born on October 21, 1942, a cold gray Oregon morning. My entrance into this world was watched by my grandparents from both sides. Early in the day they had all gone for a ride in the lush countryside. They had stopped at a small market to buy fresh salmon, the local specialty in my birthplace of Medford. Then everyone but my mother climbed back into the car.

Yaltah was slow. She was barely five feet tall, and I must have added twenty pounds to her tiny frame. As she came out of the store, Moshe drove off without her. My mom ran crazily after the car, trembling and crying because she thought her father was leaving her behind. By the time he stopped and turned back, her face was red, and she looked violently ill. Yet all Marutha could do as Yaltah crawled miserably back into the car was to insult her in Hebrew.

Later in the hospital room my mother was holding the hand of my father's mother, who was quite shocked by what she had just seen. "You are a good person, Bea," Yaltah said to her mother-in-law. "My mother, Marutha, is so cold, so very cold."

As I said, my entrance into the world was not entirely pleasant.

When I was four years old, my mother and I took the train to Los Gatos to celebrate Christmas with the elder Menuhins, as well as my uncle Yehudi. Yehudi brought me Lego and Tinker Toy sets. He got down on the floor and showed me what could be done with them. My father did not come. I think he probably was not invited.

The handsome couple early in their marriage

From left, Yaltah, Benjamin, Marutha and Lionel. From this picture you'd never know that Marutha hated her son-in-law so intensely.

Even as late as 1950, Marutha was complaining how "repulsive" Ben was to them.

Her daughter had brought me to Los Gatos for a visit.

"It was a sweet visit until she began to miss her husband, I guess, and as I am totally allergic to him and would not even mention him, she was not very pleased," Marutha wrote in a letter to family friends Esther and Al Shak.

In that same letter in 1950, mentioning how my mother had gone on a European concert tour, Marutha went on to suggest that "a happy wife does not go off for some silly concerts to Europe. So this is the way it stands. She claims she loves him and I am glad if it's true, but he is repulsive in the full sense to both of us."

Yaltah continued touring, and I remember how after she had performed in New Zealand in 1953, she tried to convince my father to move us all there.

"What will I do?" he said. "I'm an American lawyer."

"We could open a cleaner's," she said, never astute about financial realities.

Yaltah regarded the tour as "a long and very successful tour ... It was wonderful and I had much joy when Hephzibah joined me from Australia. We also spent one week at her home in Australia after it was all over."

It was in the late '40s that Yehudi rented a mansion in the Florida Everglades for a family reunion. I met Yehudi's and Hephzibah's kids, and after a few days spent in this mansion, we went home. My mom and I had come out from Los Angeles on a TWA Constellation, a curious propeller-driven plane that shuddered and shook a lot but whose odd shape made it look futuristic. Yehudi had developed an enthusiasm for Melvin Page, a pioneer in the early movement against the evils of white sugar and white flour, and he invited Page to lecture us on nutrition.

By 1947, the year Cather died, Yehudi had a persistent suitor. Diana Gould was inevitably hovering in the background wherever Yehudi was. A gawky, too-tall ballerina from "basement royalty" (her father had been a British naval commander, although he was born in Ireland), she was determined to marry an intellectual celebrity of some kind.

Her previous target had been a prominent actor who, it turned out, liked boys better than women.

My dad might be excused if he had bent the truth out of hatred for his in-laws who treated him so badly. But he was a sober-sided judge, not given to inaccuracy. He insisted that Yehudi asked him to put Diana up, to get her out

Ben, Diana and Yehudi in 1948

of his hair. And my dad insisted he saw Diana taking out her drug paraphernalia and enjoying some cocaine one night.

One of the oddest of my recollections from my childhood was riding with my mother in the family Hillman Minx, one of the most notoriously unreliable vehicles ever created. This would have been in the early '50s. My mom would take me and three or four of my neighborhood friends, and we would head out Sunset Boulevard toward the beach.

Back in those days Sunset had a couple of traffic circles, where cars could mingle and change directions.

The traffic circles disappeared a long time ago after too many Saturday night accidents, when drunks and testosterone-driven teenage boys confronted the circle and lost.

My mom was addicted to silliness. It was usually a wonderful kind of silliness, a silliness which no doubt sprang from the fact that she never had a real childhood.

That transcendent silliness is something I've sought in women ever since, I think.

The highlight of these trips always occurred when we got to a traffic circle. Yaltah would drive around and around like it was an amusement park ride. I was proud, because I had the coolest mother in the world.

Her love of driving around and around and around the traffic circle, laughing wildly, probably was reminiscent of a moment in 1933, when the Menuhins returned from Europe to their hometown of San Francisco. Yehudi was made an honorary San Francisco policeman and fireman, and as a result

Yaltah and Lionel in 1943

he got to take his sisters riding in a fire truck downtown on Market Street at 60 miles per hour, while Yaltah furiously banged the alarm.

It must have been a glorious moment in her life.

Yehudi always was her loyal older brother, even though he could sometimes be cruel to her.

When Yehudi was hobnobbing with Nehru and being photographed practicing yoga in *Life* magazine, my mother suddenly got a spill-over effect. One day in 1956 Marlon Brando called, wanting information on yoga. My mother was excited. She rarely took us to the movies, but she had just taken us to see "Sayonara" and "Teahouse of the August Moon."

Indira Devi was one of the first yoga practitioners in the country to become famous, in part because Yehudi and Gloria Swanson endorsed her work. One day Indira took me to Farmer's Market. I said I would go but I made a scene, insisting that I didn't want to eat vegetarian -- I wanted a hamburger. She relented.

In the '50s, my mother did not sound so unhappy with my dad.

"Bud is well and as usual very sweet and helpful. I could not continue with my music if he did not share some of my duties in the house. You should see the four of us vacuuming - dusting -- shopping -- cleaning like four little children having fun pretending they keep house. It really helps to do it together," she wrote her friends, the Shaks.

There is no doubt that later my mother resented the time her children took away from her music -- and in several letters she expressed her frustration. My brother and I chattered incessantly about cars and bicycles, which we were both obsessed with. That drove her crazy, and she wished we would be interested in "human" things.

She admitted that the exuberance and mischief of her boys drove her crazy.

Still, as late as 1956, she appeared to be the dutiful wife. In a letter to the Shaks, she wrote, "I am visiting Bud's office and have been writing letters waiting for the 3 o'clock cup of coffee he treats me to when I join him downtown. He comes home for lunch every day and sometimes I drive back to work with him and keep busy while he is working ... Bud is very happy in his work and we love the leisurely lunch hour we can share with the added closeness it brings us. The boys don't give us much time or chance for adult conversation at the evening meal -- so we appreciate our 'stolen hours' at noon when we can chat freely and not be interrupted."

She added: "I enjoy them (the boys) much of the time -- except when I'm weary and they are not."

Once my mom came and spirited me away from school. We went to the airport, flew to Los Gatos, for some reason or another, and stayed in the Adolph Baller cottage at Alma, the five-square-mile estate in the Santa Cruz Mountains Yehudi acquired in the mid-'30s. The cottage was built at the same time that the main house, known as Villa Cherkess, was finally constructed. Baller had been a piano prodigy. But when he was in concentration camp, the Nazis asked him what he did. "I am a pianist," he said. They took out a ball-peen hammer and broke all his fingers.

He survived concentration camp, and eventually wound up at Stanford University where he became a great piano teacher and pedagogue.

The cottage had a library. There was one book in it that particularly struck me. It was about the Holocaust. I forgot the name, but I think it was prepared, I believe, by the United Nations. Two of its main sponsors were Albert Einstein and Yehudi Menuhin.

Back in the '50s in Long Beach, California, where we then lived, I used to get chased home through the back alleys from Woodrow Wilson High School by a gang of Christian thugs. Their leader was the son of a minister, and oh my God what a bigot was he!

The basic charge was that as a Jew, I was responsible for Christ getting killed. I guess I did it personally. That's what they seemed to be saying. Or something horrible coursed through my veins, and that horrible something was the "fact" that my Jewish ancestors had drunk the blood of Christian children.

The gang leader was, like a lot of the other Midwestern farmer-types in Long Beach, a follower of Gerald L.K. Smith, the notorious anti-Semite from the '30s.

I naturally got interested in what being a Jew meant, and like many other Jews, I read everything I could about the Holocaust and that defined me forever. My favorite novel was *It Can't Happen Here* by Sinclair Lewis. It was about fascism in America.

There in the Baller cottage I found not only the UN book, but also other books on the Holocaust that chilled and horrified me.

I discovered these books after my mother told me how Baller came to have his fingers broken.

★

One thing that should be made clear about my mother. In many ways, she never grew up. She remained a child all her life. It was a blessing and a curse, remaining the eternal child.

One could downplay the importance of Aunt Willa in my mother's life because she was mostly, although not entirely, a close childhood friend.

But my mother's whole life was, if nothing else, about her childhood. Much more than is the case with most people.

Maybe that is why the injustice of the Holocaust haunted her throughout her life.

It was not that she always cried out "Oh woe is me for I am Jewish." On the contrary, my mother never took that narrow view. She knew that many people had suffered during the war -- suffered plenty, and continue to suffer to this day, just as they had suffered for eons before. After all, six million Jews perished but more than 20 million Russians died fighting Hitler.

The war was a great watershed for her and for many others.

★

Yaltah ultimately left her family after 18 years because my father was jealous of her career, although he was torn about it. He loved the chamber music that was played in the front room of our Long Beach home, but he hated the time her touring took her away from him and their two sons. Later she married a man who dragged her down musically even more than my father ever had, and because I had agreed with her decision to leave my father, I felt a lot of ambivalence about her third husband, Joel Ryce, a Danish-Irish child prodigy musician from Sterling, Indiana.

I had supported my mother's decision to leave my dad in 1960, in part for selfish reasons. Their marriage had obviously gone sour, even though there appeared to be a lot more love and affection in it than she would admit to later.

My father painted and wrote poems which he illustrated in the style of William Blake.

He played the lute and the recorder and was regarded as one of the sharpest minds in his profession.

Before he went to law school, his only intention had been to study philosophy, but the fact that it was the Depression came home to him, so he finished his law degree.

★

Yaltah basked in the reflected glory of her famous brother. But she was rarely an accompanist. She loved chamber music most of all but still she was fiercely her own musician. With chamber music, musicians must talk to each other as equals.

That might have been why later in life her sister Hephzibah observed that Yaltah had developed musically more than she.

Marutha's injunctions against Yaltah's piano playing affected her for many years, and only when she dropped all contact with her mother did she begin to flourish.

What Marutha appeared to have given my mother was a self-defeating mechanism, as she struggled to balance her roles as a wife, a mother and a pianist. The "third child syndrome," was how Yaltah described it.

Still, she was proud of the fact that there were those -- Yehudi sometimes among them -- who said she may have been the best musician of the three.

On some level Hephzibah loved music. But mostly, music was something she used, at least later in life, as a way to raise money for her social activism. She saw herself as kind of a Robin Hood.

I once asked my mother about Hephzibah and music. I was living at Hephzibah's home at 16 Ponsonby Place, just off the Thames in London, from where she was saving the world.

It was impossible not to notice that Hephzibah, who paid for all the hustle and bustle in the house through her concerts, had only an upright in a hallway that was the main thoroughfare between the kitchen and the living room on the first of three floors.

"That's to play 'Bac'," she said, emphasizing the "a" in Bach so it sounded like "back."

It was quite different from my mother, who at the time had three grand pianos in her apartment. The pianos had belonged to Fou T'song, Yehudi's daughter Zamira's then-husband.

My mother said Hephzibah loved her music.

She was probably right, but it was a very different kind of love.

Not with intended unkindness, perhaps, Hephzibah told me that Yaltah would have been most happy married to a wealthy gentleman whose 16th century gardens she could walk in, whom she could pick roses for and write poems to.

That was part of the reason she hated seeing my mother married to Joel Ryce. There is some truth in this slighting remark, but no one denigrated Yaltah's considerable powers when it came to handling some adult matters.

Her relationship with me, her eldest son, shows that.

For many years I believed with all my heart that I had helped my mother try to find her freedom as an artist. But after her marriage to Joel, I became less convinced.

To the end of their lives, there was debate about which of the three Menuhin children was the most grown up emotionally. Yehudi's wife Diana always felt that Yaltah was hopelessly naive and childish whereas Kron, Hephzibah's oldest child, believed Yaltah became the most developed and interesting of the three.

The lack of a real childhood telescoped and reversed the childish qualities of all three siblings. Since none of the three ever had a real childhood, they remained curiously childlike.

My mother, for better or worse, spent her adult life confronting the buried issues of her childhood.

CHAPTER THREE

Breakup

My parents' divorce was fast and not friendly. It came a couple of years after an article and photo of the family -- Yaltah and Ben Rolfe and sons Lionel and Robert -- appeared in the Long Beach *Press-Telegram* in 1956. The article, ironically, was about how a woman successfully balanced her career and her family.

Even as late as 1957, on the occasion of their fifteenth anniversary, my mother said, "Bud and I are very happy. We are beginning to relax more and enjoy our fifteenth wedding anniversary."

Ultimately my mother felt that my father was holding her music back because he was jealous of her male musical colleagues.

She also resented the intensity of his hatred for the Menuhin clan, but given his history with it, there was no reason to expect anything else.

Benjamin Lionel Rolfe was born in 1914 in Minnesota, and he was proud of being a Midwesterner whose family had come to the United States in the1820s. His lineage was also different from that of the Menuhins. He was of Portuguese and German Jewish descent while she was of Russian Jewish emigré stock.

He looked down on Russian Jews. He regarded himself

as a Jewish aristocrat because he was Sephardic. His mother spoke Ladino, not Yiddish, when she grew up in a small Sephardic community around Seattle. As a kid, when I ran around without shoes, which I liked to do, he would remonstrate with me for "acting like your peasant background." When my mother got mad at him, she would tell him to take her to Canter's delicatessen in the Fairfax District, "so I can be among my people (Russian Jews)."

He was never happy when she went on a world tour, which she did several times -- a couple of times with Michael Mann, the violist son of author Thomas Mann. She also toured and played chamber music regularly with violinists Israel Baker and Eudice Shapiro, violist Paul Doktor and cellists George Neikrug, Willie Van den Berg, Howard Colf, Victor Gottlieb and Gabor Rejto, who was part of the original Alma Trio.

The duo of Menuhin-Mann ended rather abruptly early one afternoon as we were on our way to Exposition Park where the Sunday Afternoon Concerts emanated from the Natural History Museum and were heard on radio station KFAC. Mann threw a knife and a viola case at my mom and me in the back seat. Then he jumped out of the car. My unnerved father was driving. Mann went on to become a literature professor at UC Berkeley and later tried to reform their duo. Yaltah rejected the offer, just as she rejected the Mann family.

My mother was very dismissive of Thomas Mann's books which she rejected as strongly as she supported Willa's. Her experience with Michael, then with his parents, Thomas and Katia, was a negative one.

I remember her attitude was that for a man who was supposed to represent democracy and freedom, she thought that Mann's household was like a totalitarian state -- and his children were being sacrificed to his needs as a writer.

She thought he was not so different from the Nazism which he crusaded against.

Interesting enough, some critics noted that although Mann was the great writer who kept the conscience of Germany alive in exile, there was a certain totalitarian streak in him and his writing. My mother felt as if she had personal knowledge of that totalitarian streak.

After the Menuhin-Mann duo was dissolved, Katia and Thomas were concerned my mother might sue them because of the cancellation of a world tour. So Katia accused my mother of having "done something to upset Michael" and added a warning that one must never "upset a Mann."

My mother responded that "a Mann had tried to kill a Menuhin." She had no desire to sue. She just wanted nothing more to do with them.

Far earlier in the game, Willa was proud that Alfred and Blanche Knopf were publishing such great European writers as Thomas Mann, and they convinced her to write an introduction for his *Joseph and His Brothers*.

Willa met Thomas Mann only once, and not much is known about that meeting. Willa developed an intense appreciation of his work, but she excluded the work that came out of his fight against Nazism.

She loved *Joseph and His Brothers* in part because he was writing a kind of history, just as she did. In the case of the Mann book, it was biblical history.

She pointed out that everyone knows the story -- the writer is not going to be able to use "bizarre invention" to hold the reader. The power, she said, is in having "the old story brought home to us closer than ever before ... Shakespeare knew this act very well, and the Greek dramatists long before him."

Willa said that the "story of *Joseph and His Brothers* is not only forever repeated in literature, it forever repeats itself in life." In an essay she wrote in 1936, she talked about Mann's technique of storytelling which involved use of a peculiar kind of time machine.

"With a sense of escape we approach something already known to us; not glacier ages or a submerged Atlantis, but the very human Mediterranean shore, on a moonlight night in the season of Spring," she wrote.

She said the story was driven by a search for "a God who was not a form, but a force, an essence, felt but not imprisoned in matter."

In her essay on Mann's *Joseph* Cather makes a remark that is more revealing than one might think about the book she has just finished -- *Lucy Gayheart*. A disturbing part of the novel, as we will discuss later, was whether Lucy's death was by design or circumstance.

Referring to Mann's Joseph in *Joseph and His Brothers*, she says that "he knows that even external accidents often have their roots, their true beginnings, in personal feeling."

She proves her point by saying that "he accepts the evidence of the bloody coat and believes that Joseph was devoured by a boar or a lion, yet his glance at the brothers is always accusing. But for their hatred, the wild beast might not have come down upon Joseph."

I remember telling my mother, whose dislike of Mann was quite complete, that whatever she thought of him he was, in fact, a great writer, and *Doctor Faustus* was one of the greatest, if not the greatest, works of the 20th century.

Significantly, she listened without comment.

I think another person who ranked high on my mother's list was Josef Szigeti, the great violinist who, like Yehudi, had premiered the works of Béla Bàrtók, the man some think was the greatest composer of the 20th century. I think Yaltah admired Szigeti, who like Bàrtók was Hungarian, in the same way she loved Cather, although she had known Cather better as a child and she was an adult when she performed with Szigeti, who by that point was an elderly man. She was tremendously excited to be playing Beethoven's Kreutzer Sonata with Szigeti.

We always looked forward to going to Szigeti's house. I was almost always along, sometimes turning pages for my mom under Szigeti's watchful eye.

By that time, Szigeti had lost much of his technique, but like Pablo Casals in his later years, the quality of his interpretation shone through his defects. My mother was always quite angry that Jascha Heifetz had once invited Szigeti to play a benefit for his students at USC -- and one of the reasons he was invited was so that Heifetz and his friends and students could laugh at how the old man's playing had deteriorated.

She thought it was cruel and unfair, and showed the pettiness that Heifetz often displayed in private, which some partisans argue showed through in his otherwise magnificent playing.

Although my mother saw the clay feet of people like Heifetz (and Mann), it did not keep her from working with them musically. One of my mom's closest collaborators in chamber music, with whom she toured, was Israel Baker, who was one of Heifetz's greatest students.

I was often at my mother's side when she went to rehearse, to perform or simply to play chamber music with other musicians. I turned pages for her. She seemed to value my opinions, if they weren't offered too vociferously.

I remember that one year on my birthday, we went into a recording studio and she recorded all the Chopin Preludes.

For my mother, that was a perfect birthday present -- and it also seemed that way to me.

However, at the studio, the engineer tried to tell her how to play. Her reaction was quite direct. She told him that she was the musician and he was the engineer and never the two would mix. His job was faithfully to record whatever she played, no more, no less. I can't help wondering how she would regard the current trend toward "hands-on" producers in the world of classical recordings.

I wish I still had that recording of the twenty-one Preludes. Somehow it got lost during those many years I knocked around after my parents' split.

What did not get lost so quickly were memories of my mom's emotional rhythms. The day of a concert I learned to stay out of her way. She was always taut and nervous. Some performers become inured to nerves before a concert, but this was rarely the case with her.

I think my dad became upset over two things. It was hard for a man to run a family and work while the other partner, his wife, was away on a world tour. He was also jealous. My sense is that he needn't have been, but children often are the last to have an accurate sense of their parents' sex life.

I paid heavily in later years for supporting my mother. My father and I had a rocky relationship that became closer only at the end, because he blamed me for encouraging her to leave. He never recovered from her leaving. I believe he loved her a lot.

By the time I was 16, I spent very little time at my father's place. My mom had moved into a nearby old apartment building on Bronson and Franklin in Hollywood.

One time I, my dad and Robby came to sleep overnight on the floor of her small apartment. I was particularly proud of the new car -- a Mini-Minor -- that my father had bought me.

"They shoved me into their new car ... glad to have such a toy, when to make ends meet I had to sell my beautiful piano. But I know that to a man ... to a boy ... a car is a symbol of some power," my mom later recalled.

I began my student life, living around coffeehouses and radical politics. At that point, my mother moved to New York and then to London.

My father definitely distanced himself from me during this period. I lived in squalid student housing and when I couldn't pay the rent, I fled to sleep on someone's couch. I was reading all the time -- Dostoevsky and Tolstoy in particular.

My own history with music was a mixed blessing. I think that I felt terribly inadequate as a musician, even though I had started, in the tradition, playing at a young age.

My mother was my first teacher on the piano, but it quickly became apparent to both of us that this was not going to be successful, so she put me in other hands, but it evidently wasn't meant to be. After the piano I took a few violin lessons, first in a public school and then with a violinist who was the first chair in the Los Angeles Philharmonic.

I studied the classical guitar for several years, although I felt like a bit of a fraud because I never really learned how to read music well. I had to suffer through each piece, even the simplest of the Bach preludes transcribed for guitar by Segovia, almost learning them by memory.

Nonetheless, Raul Gripenwaldt, the music critic for the

Santa Monica *Outlook* and an impresario around town, set up some sort of performance after my mother played at a high school. I had already played for regular meetings of the lute and guitar club my father and I went to.

On this occasion I nervously plunked through the piece, without any great fault, and thought I had acquitted myself adequately but not tremendously. However, I judged the applause to be only grudging.

Despite high praise from my mom and Gripenwaldt, I gave up then and there, and have not played the guitar since.

I knew the truth. I did not play with enough facility or technique to offer anything in the way of interpretation. It just didn't come together for me as it did for the Menuhin children. I'm surprised my mother could not see that -- and

About the time this picture was taken, Lionel gave a concert on the classical guitar and decided he didn't want to end up being a second-rate Menuhin.

I think it was good that I moved away from performing music.

I next toyed with the idea of making films. I was going to be the next Eisenstein or Fellini, until I realized that the art of transforming your vision into a film has more to do with your fundraising abilities than anything else.

When I finally got around to writing my first book, *The Menuhins,* I felt as if I were also composing music. I didn't succeed with that book so brilliantly as Cather had in *My Antonia,* where you can hear a symphony in her words. Still, I'm still convinced if I had been able to write down the music I felt inside of me, I might have been a fair composer. But my decision to get away from music was probably inevitable.

Despite my mother's hopes for me as a musician, I did not want to be a second-rate Menuhin. Besides, I deeply suspected that I would be a better writer than a musician. At the same time I knew that my mother looked down on writers. She didn't like raconteurs. She equated the two. "Oh, he's nothing but a talker," she might say about someone she didn't trust.

So I was determined to become a writer. I got very politically involved -- and finally ended up writing for the *People's World* (the communist newspaper), and the Los Angeles *Free Press* (the first underground newspaper), which made its national appearance in Los Angeles in the '60s. My father was horrified, being an old mainstream Roosevelt Democrat. Soon many of the lawyers who appeared before him told him what good articles I was writing. He was impressed with this fact.

★

My mother had imbued me, in many ways, with the attitudes if not the actual education of a 16th century gentleman. I believed in the ethos of the artist above all else. The businessman -- commerce and finance in general -- was on the lowest rung in my mother's scheme of things, and hence in my scheme of things as well.

So she left my father, left me, left my brother, and married Joel Ryce, another pianist, in much the same way her sister Hephzibah also left her children, left Australia, and went to London to marry a penniless social activist and concentration camp survivor. This was after having been part of Australia's wealthiest families.

★

Maybe Willa Cather was not entirely blind to Marutha's faults, because she once counseled Yaltah not to leave my father and to stand up to her parents -- which, in particular, meant facing off with Marutha, who could be a very formidable woman. One of the reasons Yaltah was attracted to Willa was because her words made sense. They were meaningful, as opposed to the crazy fantasy world represented by her mother.

Yaltah read and reread Willa's books all her life, getting more out of them each time. She devoured Willa's books the way she devoured a musical score, minutely yet with passion.

But if my mother's parents held her back, and then her husband, my father, also held her back, her third husband ended up being the biggest impediment of all her musical career.

It was only after her third husband died that she began to emerge on the concert stage again. It may even be that she was miserably lonely and depressed by his death, seeking solace in music -- yet in the last three years left to her after he died, she underwent something of a musical rebirth.

Willa Cather's female protagonists were survivors. Yaltah

survived and triumphed perhaps because Cather's protagonists were so ingrained in her.

CHAPTER FOUR

Not Just Some Crazy Aunt

I had read some of Willa's books, and I was particularly taken by *Death Comes for the Archbishop*. Later in life when I began to write about writers, I was too busy focusing on California bohemian writers like Samuel Clemens and Jack London, to go off on a tangent about my mother's "Aunt Willa." I was also taken with left-wing writers, and Willa was one of those who railed on against FDR.

There was even a tinge of racism in some of her writings, especially before she got to know people of other races. She was a product of her times, for better or for worse.

Willa loved tradition, in religion and in culture. Although she was not a Catholic, she was attracted to the trappings of tradition in Catholicism. That is why she was able to produce a book much beloved by Catholics: *Death Comes to the Archbishop*.

But she had bohemian links as well. For example, Cather had a friendship with Mary Austin, the histrionic but talented writer who was part of the California bohemian movement, especially when Austin was in residence at the Carmel colony which became its headquarters after the 1906 San Francisco earthquake.

It was only many years later that I began to realize that my mother's "Aunt Willa" was not just some crazy aunt. She was an incredible artist and writer with a profound, if not easily analyzed, connection to music. Willa was no musical snob. She loved a wide range of music, from the music made by the itinerant Mexican workers who lived with their families on the plains in the 19th century, to opera and chamber music. For instance, she wrote a particularly powerful account of a black "jazz" pianist, performing. But she first loved opera and then as a result of her friendship with the Menuhins, at least in part, she came to love chamber music.

As I was writing this book, and was assembling my Cather books and papers, an amazing coincidence struck me. I discovered that I had used a couple of Cather's story titles in my own writing about pivotal events in my life without realizing where they may have come from. I had written about a place I always called "The Bluff," whereas she wrote about "An Enchanted Bluff" in the Southwest desert. I also wrote, as she had, about a "Death in the Desert" in a couple of chapters in my book *Fat Man on the Left: Four Decades in the Underground*. They were not the same stories, but the similarity of the titles astonished me. I remember feeling smug at having come up with such good titles, only to then realize I had not just pulled them out of the air.

It was not easy thinking that "Aunt Willa" was also a great writer. References to her were so commonplace in my home that I felt her presence in nearly everything connected to my mother.

To my mother, Willa Cather was the woman who had taught her what art was, what being an artist meant, and what the search for Truth was about -- whether on the piano or typewriter keyboard.

Shortly before she died my mother and I had a surprisingly acrimonious and personal argument considering the subject.

She had apparently been disappointed most of her life that I did not continue studying the classical guitar. She felt I was good at it -- a conclusion with which I disagreed.

My mother adamantly insisted that words can never convey great depth and move one emotionally and intellectually in the way that music can. They cannot duplicate the rapture of a great musical moment.

"What good does talking and arguing do?" she asked me. She looked meaningfully at me, since I am indeed given to talking and arguing sometimes.

"What about people who use words like Aunt Willa did?" I shot back.

I reminded her that Aunt Willa used words, and that her words had often had melody and rhythm in the same way an orchestra does.

My mother had no answer to this, and she obviously was thinking about the implications of what I'd said.

It makes me sad that my mother and I never really finished our conversation about words and music, which would have allowed us to get beyond the anger and personal disappointments to the thing itself.

But the simple truth was that she put music on the highest plain of human endeavor, and pegged everything else on a lower level.

On the occasion when my mom and I last argued, I wished I had asked her more about what made Willa's writing as elevated as music. I know she would have had an interesting answer.

Words, like notes, have sounds, colorations, are short and brutal or long and lingering. There is physics and arithmetic in harmony not normally easily communicated in writing. Yet somehow Willa had music in her writing.

Cather's role as a teacher to the Menuhin children was quite specific. She introduced literature into the "curriculum" side by side with music.

And in the process, the music no doubt fed Willa; and her literature affected the music. To interpret a piece of music, it is mandatory to know the Zeitgeist -- the ideas, passions, institutions and habits of a specific era. Understanding literature helped the children understand the music they played. In Willa's case, she put the music into her writing.

Certainly writing is not so abstract as music, although words, of course, do have shape and melody and color and even harmony of their own -- at least in a few authors. Writing usually comes out of the real world, and for the Menuhins, Cather was happy to put away her characters and work her magic on them instead.

Willa was never fond of Lucy Gayheart, for example, the character she created in the novel by the same name. Yaltah was seeing a great deal of Willa when she was writing *Lucy*, much more so than her brother or sister. Willa loved all of them, however, and had strong relationships with Yehudi and Hephzibah as well. Her love of the children was also made all the more intense by the fact she was getting no joy from her writing. She wrote by hand and then a secretary typed up the manuscript. She was in constant pain with a wrist ailment.

Lucy was a young pianist not quite able to come to terms with life and love in the big city or the little town.

The book was important among Cather's work, even if it didn't quite have the power of some of her earlier books.

Cather was revisiting old themes with Lucy. In *The Song of the Lark*, published in 1915, Thea Kronberg was a musician who left the plains and went to the big city. Lucy did not have the grit and substance of Thea, however, and the contrast between the two is fascinating. Lucy was not a great musician, but she was some kind of intense life force.

In much the same way that Willa was often the voice of the narrator in her books, she also was part of Yaltah's internal life.

Perhaps Yaltah was Willa Cather's greatest character -- not a character she had created on paper, but a character she molded in real life. Forget *My Antonia*, or *Lucy Gayheart* or *The Song of the Lark*. These and other books like *O Pioneers!* or *Death Comes for the Archbishop* were only that -- fiction. Everything Yaltah came to believe, and her lifelong struggle as a musician, was inspired by the teachings of her mentor Aunt Willa.

One wonders if Willa pondered the difference between the flesh and blood Yaltah and the character Lucy, who were both with her at the same time, and that is why she felt so much frustration with Lucy.

The intensity of the relationship between the two was brought back to me on an occasion in the early 1980s when my mother gave me Aunt Willa's letters to sell.

"Aunt Willa would have wanted me to give them to you because she would have supported your struggles as a writer," she told me when she mailed them to me in Los Angeles from London.

I was exceptionally broke at the time and what Yaltah did floored me. She didn't even insure the letters -- she just mailed them in an ordinary envelope -- letters, as it turned out, that were worth thousands of dollars.

I was shocked because scholars had been beseeching her for years to be allowed to read the letters. She kept them in a shoe box in a closet in London. She never let the academics read them, for she respected Willa's desire that no one should ever read her letters. But after Cather's partner Edith Lewis died, I guess her thoughts changed.

"Willa would have approved," she said. "You were the one who saved those letters when I divorced your father," she said.

★

One morning -- sometime in the late 1950s -- my mom and I were walking through Central Park and she pointed up at a beautiful old building. She told me it was where Aunt Willa had lived with Edith Lewis, her companion.

I asked Yaltah if she thought Willa was a lesbian, as had been rumored.

My mother said she didn't think so. But of course she met Aunt Willa in Paris when the author was approaching fifty and she was under ten years of age -- an age when the peculiarities of sexual attraction are not well understood.

Of course Yaltah was becoming an adolescent during the most intense parts of her friendship with Willa, but my mother kept an adolescent naivety right up until the end of her life.

I didn't ask my mother more about Aunt Willa's putative lesbianism, perhaps because as a son I never saw my mother as someone who would understand sexual attraction anyway.

Also, despite the fact Willa wrote so well about strong women, I thought she also wrote well about men and women. She just didn't write about them with a lot of sentimentality.

Others say she hardly wrote about sex at all. But there was a lot of sensual and even erotic writing in *O'Pioneers!* and *My Antonia*.

My mother's attitude towards homosexuality was complex. She had met the artists Frank Ingerson and George

Dennison in Paris at the same dinner table and about the same time as she met Willa. Frank and George later lived at Cathedral Oaks in California's Santa Cruz Mountains.

She left me with Frank and George for a couple of days on more than one occasion -- days which I loved. Cathedral Oaks (later to become part of Yehudi's Alma estate) was a grand woodsy place in a grove of tall trees. I knew Frank and George were a "married" couple, but I was never told to be afraid of them -- and I wasn't and, as it turned out, had no reason to be.

On the other hand, part of the reason my mother came to resent and diminish the importance of the great author Thomas Mann was because of his trumpeting of homosexuality as a superior lifestyle. She did not feel it necessarily was.

"It was a belittling of the bourgeoisie, people who have children," she said.

She did not seem to put Willa's relationship with Edith Lewis in the same category as that of Frank and George. And if she did, it struck her as simply part of the natural order of things.

It's not that my mother was a prude. Later in life, when I was in my early teens, I developed a friendship with a girl that had begun when we were both in elementary school. We used to go into a shed behind my parents' garage and take our clothes off, and then not do much more because we didn't know what else we were supposed to be doing.

My mother knew something was going on, but she didn't stop us. As a youngster, she had been raised with no knowledge of sex, and perhaps she didn't want me to grow up that way.

For her, Willa's sexuality never was a matter of any concern.

CHAPTER FIVE

Aunt Willa's World

I read two of Aunt Willa's greatest and most memorable books, *O Pioneers!* and *Death Comes for the Archbishop*, when I was in my early teens.

It was when I was much older and I read *My Antonia*, *The Song of the Lark* and *Lucy Gayheart* that I had something of a revelation.

Willa Cather's descriptions of the wilderness of Nebraska and Colorado, and the desert of the Southwest, before cars, electricity, phones or even roads and towns, is more like hearing a symphony than reading a simple narrative. Her prairie was magical and colorful, full of motion and mystery, expressed in melodic prose that swells and falls. Her words are deceptively simple, but they are also haunting and powerful and much more descriptive, in my humble opinion, than the music of Copland, for example.

Cather herself was explicit, believing that "a novel should be like a symphony, developed from one theme, one dominating tone."

The Menuhins became important to her if for no other reason than the force of their youthful energy. By the time she began writing *Lucy Gayheart* in the '30s, something had gone out of her. Her fellow Midwestern writer, Hamlin Garland, who saw her at that time, wrote that she had aged considerably. She had become a "plain, short, ungraceful, elderly woman ... (who) spoke without force or grace, with awkward gestures." But he noted she still wrote beautiful things.

And that must have been her allure to the Menuhin children. Garland saw the sad and tired side of her, but either she hid that from the children, or took such great delight in their presence that it simply vanished from her face when she was with them.

Hephzibah once remarked that she read later that Cather was quite depressed during the period the children spent so much time with her -- about the time she was writing *Lucy*. But she said Aunt Willa never seemed cross or grumpy when she was with them.

Yaltah's whole understanding of the artist, particularly of the woman artist, came from Aunt Willa, and would affect me dramatically in the young part of my own life.

Just as Thea in *The Song of the Lark* does not discover who she is until she realizes that her connection with the land is her true source of strength, so that same connection with the land was, by the testimony of all three Menuhins, emphasized in their art as a result of knowing Cather.

You wouldn't think that a sense of place would be so important in music, which is the most abstract of all arts, divorced it would seem from the physical plane of life. But if you think about it, composers always wrote programmatic music about landscapes.

For some reason, I could listen to Smetana's "The Moldau" over and over. I have traveled that river journey more times than I would care to count. When I was 14, Wagner's stormy skies and magnificent meadows and mountains were all that seemed there was of the world when I would walk down the street, forgetting that I was in the city, so filled was my head and heart with his pounding chords and soaring melodies.

Perhaps that had begun with that sense of place Cather gave my mother. Even when Cather hated Nebraska, she knew her attachment to "the shaggy grass country" had gripped her with a passion she had never been able to shake.

"It has been the happiness and curse of my life," Cather wrote.

"There was nothing but land; not a country at all, but the material out of which countries are made ... I had the feeling that the world was left behind, that we had got over the edge of it, and were outside man's jurisdiction," Cather's protagonist says in *My Antonia*.

Cather was that "real American" the Menuhin children had to know. Whether her heroines escaped or stayed on the land, it was always the land that was primal. Then came the towns and cities that sprang from the land. And her characters had typically come from other lands as well, to which they had primal attachments. That, too, was a classic theme of Cather's.

For Cather, the Menuhin children represented the European sophistication she had always sought. Although she was an intensely American writer, Cather was also an expatriate. She wrote about Europe, but always through the prism of America.

★

The Song of the Lark was published in 1915, more than fifteen years before its author met the Menuhins.

In a copy of *The Song of the Lark* that Yaltah gave Joel, her third and last husband, she wrote an inscription saying it was from "his skylark."

There is no doubt that Yaltah related to Willa's characters. As Willa wrote, she discussed what she was writing with Yaltah. What is for sure -- Thea in *The Song of the Lark* is a much different musician than *Lucy Gayheart*.

Might she have borrowed part of the Menuhin personalities for *Lucy*? -- and Yaltah's in particular?

Edith Lewis notes this could have been true. For one thing, having the Menuhin children around all the time plunged Cather back into the world of classical music in which she thrived.

"It could be that her meetings with Yehudi during 1930 and 1931 and her return to Red Cloud after her mother Virginia Cather's death combined to produce the idea for *Lucy Gayheart* (1935)," Lewis said. But she added there had been at least two other prototypes for *Lucy* as well.

In my view all the factors -- including the Menuhin kids -- contributed.

So it was not surprising that Lewis herself admitted that it may have been the atmosphere of music the Menuhin children had brought into her life that inspired Cather to write *Lucy Gayheart*, which is about a pianist who is a practice accompanist to a great singer. Lucy, of course, falls in love with the singer. It was inevitable she would have fallen in love with a singer.

Cather's first major musical character was Thea from *The Song of the Lark*. If anyone would have been fascinated by the children, Cather was one who most particularly would have been drawn to them. After all, here were three prodigies, the eldest a boy with immense talent. But the sisters were also nearly as prodigious.

Lucy, written some years later, was the second major musical protagonist Cather created. Lucy had elements of Yaltah or Hephzibah in her characterization, but certainly not of Yehudi. Thea was more like Yehudi -- but again, Cather wouldn't have known that because he was born a year after the novel was published.

According to differing accounts, Cather was also thinking of dedicating *Shadows on the Rock*, published in 1931, to the Menuhins because the book came out shortly after she first met them in Paris. But she was talked out of it twice by family friend Sammy Marantz, who convinced her that doing so would be considered a great transgression by Moshe and Marutha -- especially Marutha.

She had already written the intended dedication: "For Yehudi, Hephzibah and Yaltah." She later added a stern reminder to the printer, "This is off, understand." She didn't want the dedication inadvertently included.

Could Cather have subconsciously borrowed from Yaltah in her *Lucy Gayheart* character?

Lucy was not a great artist. Rather, she was an accompanist to a great opera singer and appeared to be content to remain so.

She just wanted to be in his presence. Cather wrote about people who were not necessarily performers, but just wanted to be in the presence of artists. Her 1903 story "Paul's Case" was an extreme example of this. One felt that she heavily identified with Paul, who committed suicide rather than face a mundane, lower middle class life without music and art.

Perhaps Willa felt some kinship with Yaltah in all this, for although Yaltah played, it was mostly chamber music with other musicians -- and not public solo engagements, as her brother and sister were doing.

Did Willa see the depth of Yaltah early on? Perhaps the frustration she had with Lucy as a character was a sense that she was a silly girl, but there was also the suspicion that she was more than a mere talent, she was the life force itself.

Maybe this made it possible for Willa to borrow a bit of Yaltah for Lucy -- I know that sometimes as I read *Lucy Gayheart* I almost felt the presence of my mother as a young woman.

I know that I had a somewhat similar experience when I researched and wrote about Thomas Mann, who was finishing *Doctor Faustus* shortly before my mother began touring with Michael, Thomas' violist son.

There was a character named Nepomuk, or Echo, an angelic child who appears in the last part of *Doctor Faustus*. I told my mother that I had an odd feeling I knew Nepomuk.

"You did know him," she said. "You remember Michael's son, who gave me the mumps that time, don't you?" my mother asked. "He was such a nice, quiet boy; today he is a theologian in Germany. I saw him not long ago in Zurich."

Similarly, as I read *Lucy*, I felt as if there was something incredibly familiar about her.

I think now I was feeling my mother's presence.

Even if a strong musical consciousness had not been present in Willa's writings, there were other elemental themes in Willa's writing that would have fascinated Yaltah and the other two children.

At the heart of the Menuhin legend was the paradox of a strangely European musical phenomenon blossoming out of the Wild West. Surely it was not an accident that Cather wrote about the Old West as well. There was a lot of the Wild West left in San Francisco in the 1920s. Louis Persinger, Yehudi's first important teacher, had played for Colorado miners in the late 19th century.

But when Yehudi needed to progress in his career, Europe was the only choice.

Still, the friendship was renewed in New York and it deepened.

Willa was Yaltah's main inspiration throughout her life, consciously so as she struggled to continue her art, chafing under what she considered an oppressive and jealous husband, my father, as well as overbearing parents.

At the time I shared my mother's vision both of what an artist is and of her own particular situation. Willa wrote about strong women, weak women, women who were farmers as well as great musicians. I don't think I realized then whose ideas my mother was promulgating.

Aunt Willa is generally credited as being one of the first novelists to write about women who follow their own muse -- women as artists rather than as mothers and wives.

Thea in *The Song of the Lark* is the best example of this. She knew there was no room for a significant other if she was "married" to her muse. Before that, women in fiction had been characters only insofar as they were mothers, lovers and wives.

When my mother left, I remained behind with my father. Our relations were strained because he blamed me for siding with her.

At that point, I did not understand the effect "Aunt Willa" had on me through my mother. Perhaps I thought I was just siding with my mother -- but in retrospect I think I was siding with Willa through my mother.

As I said, my mother kept expressing her gratitude that I had saved her Willa Cather letters and books and gave them to her when my parents broke up their household.

Yet I suffered because of my mother's career aspirations, just as Thea's lover Fred did because of Thea's career in *The Song of the Lark*.

I lost a mother. I might have lived a fairly privileged life if my parents had stayed together. Even then, I felt as if I was stepping aside so my mother could grow.

As time went on, I came to see my dad's concerns as well.

Which is not to say that what she did was wrong, even if it caused a great deal of pain.

★

In *The Song of the Lark* Thea's parents decide they have to discuss how to raise their daughter. They have to weigh the development of her gifts against the needs of the rest of the family.

Thea is about to embark on her last year of school when her beloved first piano teacher departs. Thea is a good teacher, and she debates quitting school and making a living teaching her piano teacher's students.

Her father, a minister, says she could make a better, more reliable living giving music lessons than teaching in a country school.

Both parents realize that Thea was too serious ever to have a childhood, that she was destined to be independent and was not the "marrying kind."

"If you don't want her to marry Ray, let her do something to make herself independent," her father tells the mother in arguing that she should become a piano teacher, and he offers to build an extra room onto the house for her.

The only objection from her mother is that Thea should have some time to contemplate her future without taking on great responsibilities, of whatever kind. She'll be tied down soon enough whatever happens, her mother points out.

But the logic of the father's suggestions prevails, and Thea is glad to quit school anyway.

In a very real sense Moshe and Marutha with Yehudi were like Thea's parents were with their daughter, whose talent, they knew, was literally out of their world. Thea's parents knew she was more special than they probably could appreciate. And while they loved all their children, they knew that Thea was unusually intelligent and special.

They knew someday she would go far.

The world of the plains was a world of railroads and farms, not art and great music. There were a couple of people in the town who had a glimmer of art, but a limited one. One was Thea's old German music teacher (Willa had had just such a teacher and mentor, whom we'll talk about later), and the other was Doctor Archie, who believed in Thea but didn't quite understand what he was believing in.

One special night Doctor Archie and the very young Thea get in a conversation while watching some rabbits running in the moonlight. It was a hauntingly beautiful moment as the doctor talked to her of a larger world. He was as high-minded a man as there was in Moonstone (Willa's hometown of Red Cloud), but he knew Thea was on an entirely different level than he was. He didn't know what Thea would one day become, but he was sure she would one day make her mark in the larger world out there.

Thea's father was a minister and her mother a minister's wife. Moshe Menuhin ran several Hebrew School campuses in San Francisco, so appearances were important to both.

Thea's parents' decision to arrange for her to quit school and become a full time music teacher was similar to Moshe's contemplations about the difficulties of keeping his own career in light of his peculiarly talented offspring. Taking his family to Europe so that Yehudi, and his daughters, whether by design or not, would get a first rate musical education, was the necessary first step.

For the minister, he had only to rearrange his house, which was not a simple task, but one he plainly was capable of. Also, while Thea's sisters and brothers had no talents to match hers, that most certainly was not the case with the Menuhins.

Moshe and Marutha proudly proclaimed that only one of their children was destined for the concert stage, yet even Yaltah was not denied music and piano lessons.

If Yaltah affected Willa's *Lucy Gayheart*, Thea Kronberg was probably the Willa Cather character who most affected my mother.

Toward the end of *The Song of the Lark*, Thea talks about the essential loneliness of the touring life. As the art develops, the inner life wilts.

The artist in Thea who has risen to great heights and found that she has sacrificed her personal life, makes another terrible discovery.

She was more the all-consumed artist when she was a child than she is as a mature woman. She tells Doctor Archie, who accompanied her on her first trip to Chicago when she was a child looking for musical guidance, that she had had a rich romantic past at that point. "I had lived a long, eventful life, and an artist's life, every hour of it."

Now she's not so sure she lives that full artist's life anymore. She feels a terrible emptiness in her personal life -- even though that can be lost by focusing on her current artistic strivings, she admits to Archie.

★

I found a marked up copy of *Willa Cather: A Critical Biography* by E.K. Brown among my mother's belongings which were sent to me after her death.

In particular she noted the passages about how Willa

always sought out the dreamers and nonconformists in Red Cloud in defiance of the "tight" and "mean" ways of the American early pioneer stock that predominated in Nebraska in the 1880s. Her work was dominated by the dichotomy she saw between the pioneers and artists, and the similarities thereof, which was why the Menuhins came to love her and she, them.

Also, Cather was drawn to artists, the unconventional and even the rebels (the soft spot she had for Emma Goldman, the "red" anarchist, illustrates this), but a major part of her life, as she saw it, was promulgating traditional values as well -- in music, in politics and in religion.

Yaltah underlined this passage from *The Song of the Lark*: "What was any art but an effort to make a sheath, a mold in which to imprison for a moment the shining, elusive element which is life itself ...?"

Willa struggled with that part of her which was a pioneer, and it was a considerable part, and with her more worldly self. Antonia in *My Antonia* may have struggled to become a pioneer farmer, but Willa credited her struggle as much as she did Thea's struggle, which was to leave the plains and go to the city where culture is created and conquer it.

Antonia was as creative as Thea. She is creating something -- a farm, which can be as difficult to do as to sing an opera. In a very real way, she was writing about claustrophobia and release.

Willa wrote about the plains, and then she wrote about America and Europe and European exiles, of which she was one. Yaltah had sunderlined a part in Brown's book in which it is noted that Willa first went to Paris in 1902.

Yaltah also underlined a part in the Brown book that talks about Willa consoling Jan Hambourg for the loss of their beloved mutual friend, his wife Isabelle, in 1938 by saying that for people like them, their time had come and gone and there is "no future at all for people of my generation." Willa wrote then with intensity to record "her memories while there was yet a little time."

The crux of Willa's work was that it looked backward. She was not an observer of contemporary political or cultural doings, and it was just as well, because her politics were quite conservative.

CHAPTER SIX

The Biblical Menuhins

illa Cather had been dubious about the legitima-cy of musical prodigies until she met the Menuhins, sometimes known as the "Biblical Menuhins." Perhaps because she herself could never have been a musical prodigy, that made the real thing in the form of a whole family of them the more compelling.

Yehudi was regarded as the greatest musical prodigy of the 20th century, and perhaps the greatest musical prodigy since Mozart. Yehudi gave his first concert when he was six, and in 1927 played the Beethoven Violin Concerto -- the greatest and certainly one of the most difficult works in the violin literature -- in Carnegie Hall at 11.

It seemed that he was born to play the violin. His parents used to take him to San Francisco Symphony concerts. The little boy was so taken with the sound of the violin he demanded a violin of his own. His parents gave him one, but he threw it down on the ground and stomped on it when he found out they had given him only a toy.

His grandmother paid for a real violin and the rest, as they say, is history.

What struck everyone about his playing was the profundity of his performance. It was as if a wise old man was playing. It was on the occasion of the Carnegie Hall recital that

The Biblical Menuhins, sometime in the early '20s. Yaltah is the baby.

Einstein made his famous remark about Yehudi having convinced him there was indeed a God in heaven. Willa was also in that audience and was similarly affected.

Yehudi was given most of the encouragement by the elder Menuhins, but Hephzibah, and especially Yaltah, got far less support, even though their talents were also large. The impetus for this came from Marutha rather than Moshe. If anything, Moshe (also known as Abba, which is father in Hebrew) was always there for Yaltah intellectually, and emotionally to the extent he could be.

He just happened to be a weak man married to a very strong and ruthless woman.

Hephzibah's music was tolerated because she was Yehudi's accompanist -- and seemed to have no aspirations beyond that. Later in life Hephzibah regarded music as little more than a way to raise money for her various social concerns. She herself admitted to me that Yaltah had always been by far the more dedicated musician.

Yaltah said she was actively discouraged from the piano by Marutha, who felt that she ought to be content cooking, scrubbing and sewing for her brother and sister. Although she began playing at three, and her impromptu recitals with some of the world's top musicians in France astounded everyone, her parents never let her make any important concert appearances.

She did perform on a recording with her brother when she was 17, but that was only because Hephzibah had married and gone to Australia. It wasn't until 1950 that she appeared as a soloist with the San Francisco Symphony.

Some of Marutha's attitude toward her youngest daughter may be explained by the fact that the last time Moshe made love to his wife was when Yaltah was conceived. She was born on October 7, 1921 in San Francisco.

Yaltah said that the strong-willed Marutha believed her destiny was to give birth to a genius. She succeeded in giving birth to three of them.

Marutha never hid from her daughter the fact that she had been an unwanted child. Yehudi later said Marutha's unhappiness with Yaltah was the result of her wanting another son, but I find it hard to imagine that either Marutha or Moshe wanted to be distracted by another boy who was not a Yehudi.

Yaltah more than once compared her mother's relationship with her husband as one that a black widow (violin spider?) has to its mate, whom she devours once his work is through.

Yaltah was named after the town on the Black Sea that Marutha said her mother had come from, although because Yaltah looked a bit more like Moshe than Marutha, Marutha nicknamed her "Jerusalem," and that was not entirely an endearment.

On the whole, though, Marutha was consistent, so much so that the dogs that completed the Menuhins' early San Francisco households were named after Circassian towns, such as Alupka and Alushta. For some 50 years, there were several generations of dogs named Alupka and Alushta at the Menuhin homestead.

Alupka was always a Doberman Pinscher and Alushta a German Shepherd.

Marutha was under the delusion that she was a "Tartar princess" (sometimes this evolved into an Italian princess), and would greet people wearing silken Turkish trousers, tied around her waist with a silver belt.

Her way of making her home -- especially the innermost rooms -- look like a harem out of the Arabian Nights, began early at the family's home on Steiner Street in San Francisco.

Yaltah was forever appalled when later in Paris her mother was able to furnish her quarters with exotic rugs and pasha-like cushions. She purchased many of these at "bargain prices" from Armenians fleeing Turkey, carrying all their possessions on their backs.

Her most private rooms were off limits to most people, even, to some extent, her husband. Oddly enough, she was close and trusting with children, and her grandchildren had easy access to her boudoir.

Moshe retreated to his study, where later in life he wrote peculiarly hysterical diatribes against the Jews in Palestine.

For all Marutha's prattle about a woman's place, there was a lot of unexpected role reversal. When the children were ill or felt bad, it was Moshe who did whatever comforting that was required. To Marutha, her family had only to live by one motto. No true Cherkess ever admitted to feeling poorly even if he or she was in pain. True Cherkesses (tribal people from the Caucasus mountains) did not try to escape to their rooms where they might be alone to dream.

Yehudi also was capable of being warm to his two sisters and in this way he was more like his father than his mother. There was rarely any warmth from Marutha.

Yaltah came on the scene as her brother, and then her sister, were just beginning to perform on the public stage. Yehudi was five-and-a-half years old when Yaltah was born.

Moshe had just been appointed superintendent of the city's Hebrew schools -- which were thriving then in San Francisco -- and the family lived in an apartment at 732 Hayes Street.

Yehudi, who started going to concerts when he was

only two years old, said he remembered his mother preparing for the births of his sisters with great concern that "the life she led, the music she heard, the thoughts she had, should be part and parcel of the environment of the coming baby." Yehudi went on to say that learned doctors may argue whether this was a valid approach, but to Marutha "it was simply a truth."

A month after Yaltah was born, Yehudi gave his first public performance. It was at a recital by his violin teacher Sigmund Anker, and he played an inconsequential tune called "Remembrance." Yehudi's second public appearance was a few weeks later at a recital at a local YMCA -- he was accompanied by Marutha, who was evidently a competent accompanist, if not much more.

With the arrival of Hephzibah -- and eighteen months later Yaltah -- family life at the apartment was organized and efficient.

Marutha helped the family income by coaching Bar Mitzvah candidates and entertaining. Yehudi recalled that when Yaltah was born and Marutha was in the hospital, Yehudi's beloved teacher Louis Persinger had to drop by and tune his violin every day. Until her absence, Marutha had done it for him.

In his book *Menuhin: A Life*, Humphrey Burton suggests that this could not have been true, but Yehudi said he dutifully practiced on the Persinger-tuned violin and as a reward went to see his mother and his newborn sister Yaltah in the hospital every day until they came home.

At some point -- the exact date is unclear -- the Menuhins purchased a home at 1043 Steiner Street where they stayed until they went to Europe in 1927, when Yaltah was six years old.

Yehudi recalled that during that period Marutha often entertained, and on one of those occasions, Yaltah poured a bowl of salt into a pot where a dish was being cooked -- and she was not punished!

None of the children had any formal education. Yehudi and Hephzibah went to school for a few days. After his first day, Marutha asked Yehudi what he had learned. He said he learned nothing -- and he had missed watching the birds in the trees because the one window was raised too high. His mother agreed he should learn at home. Hephzibah lasted a few days, but her teacher ultimately pronounced her retarded. So it was obvious Yaltah would never find herself in a classroom.

The children were all highly educated from the start, however. Both parents were professional educators, who gave all of them their best. Then the best tutors that were available were hired.

A couple of their earliest French and English teachers were top professors at UC Berkeley. After Marutha, Yaltah's first piano teacher was the wife of John Paterson, a violinist in the San Francisco Symphony, who was teaching Yehudi harmony and counterpoint. All the classical subjects -- geography, philosophy and literature -- were taught, although American literature, peculiarly, was neglected until Willa came on the scene.

Moshe was their first (and last) math teacher.

The methods by which they were educated were recalled by Yehudi, who said that when he was 13, and his sisters were nine and seven, respectively, a holiday at Ospedaletti, Italy, was celebrated by daily readings from Dante's *Divine Comedy* in medieval Italian.

Moshe talked politics at the table, but Yehudi was not

encouraged to peruse the daily San Francisco papers because most of them were "puerile voyeuristic violence." But Moshe himself scoured *The New York Times*, even when he wasn't in New York, for real news about politics, science, the arts, or even such topics as adventures in the jungle or aeronautics, and he presented his children with a packet of stories every day. Indeed, to the day he died, Moshe had *The New York Times* delivered to his door, along with *The Nation*.

Moshe was a socialist at heart, whereas Marutha was quite unconcerned about social injustice, and was given to calling her children bolsheviks for their opinions, which she by no means meant as a compliment.

Breakfast discussions, lessons, walks and hikes, and sometimes diversions, usually of an "educational" nature, were the order of the day, which began early in the morning and went until early in the evening.

Yaltah had few good memories of her mother. But an exception was one morning when the two of them delivered a violin to the nearby house of Isaac Stern, the last of three prodigy violinists who emerged from San Francisco in the 1920s. (The other, besides Yehudi and Stern, was Ruggiero Ricci.)

Yehudi said the walks and hikes were organized affairs, taken every bit as seriously as their lessons in geography, literature, language, philosophy and music. Thus, he said, over the years he and his sisters got to know many of the world's great parks, from Central Park to Hyde Park to the Sydney Botanical Gardens. Their own hilly neighborhood on Steiner Street also provided adventures of various kinds.

In the scheme of things familial, Yehudi said that while Hephzibah was dependable and dutiful, Yaltah had always been fragile and wayward. He explained this by saying that Yaltah was at a disadvantage only in that Marutha had wanted a boy. Yehudi's supposition has to be juxtaposed with what Moshe told Yaltah, that she had wanted neither.

Yehudi said Yaltah's second disadvantage was that he and Hephzibah were already very much a duo, and Yaltah was often left alone.

The Menuhin clan had two alliances in the beginning. Marutha, Hephzibah and Yehudi often ganged up to tease Yaltah -- and Yaltah formed a close relationship with Moshe, who was always being bullied by his wife. Ostracism may have played a role in Yaltah's becoming the most spontaneous and unruly of the three.

Still, Yaltah loved Yehudi not just as a genius but as a God. Even when she knew his shortcomings all too well, he remained the man foremost in her life.

There had always been mixed messages in the way the Menuhins were raised. Mother and father both insisted that the daughters would not be allowed to pursue musical careers, yet they were taught "no womanly arts, whether of kitchen or drawing room, and were as helpless about the house as I was," Yehudi proclaimed.

Yehudi claims that this caused them some difficulties in their married lives -- and it is true that Yaltah's second husband, my father, was a much better cook than she was. We usually had a cook in the house, when my brother Robert and I were young.

Marutha was always in the kitchen, yet the girls were never expected to join her. Still, even in those early San Francisco days, Yaltah said she was frequently told her place was to wash clothes and cook for her brother and sister. It might have been she was told this more than she was actually instructed in it.

I think what Yehudi probably meant when he said that my

mother was too fragile for the life of a touring musician was that she always set herself up for failure. But that was something programmed into her, by her parents, her brother and her sister. And the very statement that she was too "fragile" was part of the pattern of programming that made her so "fragile."

★

There is no doubt that my mother had plenty of psychic pain growing up as one of the Menuhin prodigies. She loved her brother and sister intensely, yet she had grown up as the third and often left-out Menuhin. When the three would go walking, Yehudi and Hephzibah would hold hands and talk about man and nature and pick flowers along the way. Yaltah would bring up the rear, all by herself.

The acrimonious debate between Yaltah and Yehudi which was briefly waged in London's daily press many years later demonstrated how corrosive the relations sometimes got.

It was all about the great hair shaving incident.

When Yaltah was ten years old, Marutha shaved her daughter's head. Her golden locks fell to the floor.

Yehudi has insisted that Yaltah had so badly burned her hair while trying to make her hair look fashionable (in 1931), her mother wisely decided to cut the rest off.

Then she supposedly also cut Hephzibah and Yehudi's hair.

Another version had it that Hephzibah and Yehudi cut their own hair in protest.

Yaltah told me that Marutha was simply punishing her. Marutha was obsessed with shaving her own head and wearing wigs or turbans. She may have suffered from baldness, and she also suffered from a stubborn devotion to "principles" -- principles that seemed quite strange and even a little crazy to many outsiders.

Humphrey Burton offered another explanation.

He said that Yaltah found some hair clippers on her mother's dressing table. Marutha, he said, had arthritis that was so bad, she couldn't lift a brush to her hair. A doctor had suggested she shave her head and wear a wig.

Marutha decided that the best idea after Yaltah had hopelessly cut her long blond curls with the clippers was to shave Yaltah's scalp, saying it would do the scalp good and allow it to breathe.

At Yehudi's suggestion he and Hephzibah also shaved their heads, and were seen bathing their totally bald heads in public, looking all the while like young Tibetan monks.

Whatever the truth, there's no doubt that Marutha had a good many odd beliefs, always keeping the house in an uproar with this or that crackpot theory. One of those theories involved eating only spinach and bread. The other one was the need for baldness. Marutha insisted periodic baldness was one of her own mother's remedies for almost everything.

When Marutha invoked the name of her mother, that was invariably the end of the discussion.

The Great Shaving Incident, in my humble opinion, demonstrated a certain arbitrary irrationality peculiar to Marutha.

Yet many years later Yehudi turned his anger on Yaltah for daring to recall that memory as anything but another example of his sainted mother's perfection.

"Yaltah always loved her hair; she would sit in front of the mirror and comb her golden tresses. She still can't be separated from them, even though they now look ridiculous on her rather wizened face," Yehudi explained to a newspaper nearly fifty years later.

★

A sense of place was the key element missing in Marutha -- she never had it nor appeared to need it. Marutha was a gypsy, who could be at home anywhere. She had been vagabondizing around the earth much of her life -- often on her own, with nothing but a trunkful of costumes and her considerable wits. She was a teenager when she managed to work her way from the Crimea to London. She had already made her way to Jerusalem, where she set up shop as the local piano teacher -- even though her own favorite instrument had been cello.

A relative of Marutha -- Sonia Miller -- said she remembered Marutha at nineteen, showing up at her parents' house with nothing but her trunk full of costumes.

"Was she an actress, a prostitute? What did she live on?"

"Nobody had ever figured that out," Sonia said. "But she seemed to be able to take care of herself anywhere."

The irony is that she married a homebody, a man who ultimately found his Zion in California where he was content to live forever. And she was cruel about that difference between them, especially because her son's career required the family to go anywhere in the world, which they did.

Indeed, Moshe was offered his choice of ambassadorships -- partly because he traveled and met important people with Yehudi, and also because he had been among the first graduating class of the Herzliya Gymnasium in 1913 near what became Tel Aviv. All 21 of those original graduates went on to leadership positions in the future state of Israel, except Moshe.

In those days, Jews in what was later to become Israel were known as Palestinians. However this particular Jewish Palestinian found his Zion in California.

He needed a Zion. At the age of four, Moshe's father had

been killed by a raging mob led by priests holding up large crosses, shouting "Death to the Jews." He remembered the flames advancing up on the wall of his home in Russia -- and then, not understanding exactly what had happened, riding his tricycle around the dead body of his father where it lay outside in the morning.

Marutha had no sympathy for Moshe's emotional needs. He no doubt needed sexual affection, but he was not the kind of man to seek that satisfaction elsewhere if it were not available at home.

Marutha, meanwhile, continued chiding him mercilessly for not wanting to travel. Marutha was a self-contained human being who could make herself at home with any man, any country, so long as she ran the show.

Her husband might have become an anti-Zionist later in life, but as a youngster he had the Zionist obsession with the land. In Russia, Jews had not been allowed to own or even work the land. So a big part of the Zionist dream was that one day Jews would be allowed to own land.

When Moshe retired to Rancho Yaltah in Los Gatos in the mid-1930s, he had a five-acre orchard and garden where he also raised chickens and had a goat or two.

Despite the identical spelling, Rancho Yaltah, it had been explained to me, was not named after my mom. It was named after Marutha's birthplace on the Black Sea.

It had been many years since Moshe had set foot in a temple, but as he kept up his compost heap and prepared the soil for the fruits and vegetables he so lovingly tended, you could see his bubbling energy was that of a Hassid chanting from the God that burned constantly inside him.

He had the intense eyes of his Hasidic forbears, straining to give himself up to God even as he was delighting in the mechanics of setting a gopher trap.

Moshe found his Zion, his redemption, in the golden California hills, even more than Willa found hers in the Nebraska soil.

It was no accident that when I once asked Yehudi what had created his prodigiousness and that of his two sisters, his answer was quick and surprising. It was not a mystical call from his ancestors, nor any such thing, he said. It was simply the plentiful California sun, the wind and clean air and water and rich land of the new Zion. As he said this, I swear Yehudi's face suddenly developed that intense expression his father's got when he went to war against weeds. Pulling them out physically, one by one.

When Moshe talked and coaxed his plants to grow big and nutritious, his eyes also bulged with that strange intensity.

Moshe's intense attachment to the land was expressed in the names given to the places in and around Los Gatos where he lived. It began with Rancho Yaltah; then when the plan to build a great house in the Santa Cruz Mountains above Los Gatos was hatched, it was to be called Villa Cherkess, in honor of Marutha's obsession with being a Cherkess.

The two daughters, a bit older and more sophisticated -- in Paris (Hephzibah on the left, Yaltah on the right)

CHAPTER SEVEN

How Willa Met
The Menuhins

In my mom's opinion, Willa Cather was everything my grandmother was not. She was kind, enthusiastic, playful, and also a wise and knowledgeable woman. It was a curious journey both women took to intersect with each other.

As if anticipating her encounter with the Menuhins, Willa had written a short story in *Home Monthly* in 1897 called "The Prodigies." In it, the cruelty of a mother who pushes her prodigy children to the breaking point, causing one of them to collapse, is spotlighted. Willa herself showed no great musical abilities as a child, and perhaps this is why she was so unprepared for the Menuhins.

People assumed that because Cather could not read music or sing or play an instrument, she did not have a deep understanding of music.

Her early experiences as a music student drove her old German music teacher -- who was immortalized as the prototype for Professor Fritz Wunsch in *The Song of the Lark* -- to distraction.

"Wunsch" complained that all she wanted was to listen to music and hear about the lives of musicians. Somehow Willa developed an uncanny ability to explain the musical and personal struggles of her musician characters, without herself having any innate musical abilities. One can only wonder how someone who did not possess the magic of musical creativity could recreate it so compelling in her writing. Perhaps there is as much magic in this as there is with the five-year-old boy who picked up a violin and a short while later could plumb the depths of the Beethoven Violin Concerto.

★

Cather met the "Biblical Menuhins" in 1930 in Paris. The journey that took her to Paris had begun earlier when Willa first encountered Isabelle McClung backstage in the dressing room of the actress Lizzie Hudson Collier in Pittsburgh in 1899. Cather had already begun to achieve some fame on *The Nebraska State Journal*, writing articles about music, opera and drama. She had also written some short stories and poems. But despite a growing reputation as a journalist and an author, Cather was still living in a dreary boardinghouse and rode to her various editorial jobs on a bicycle.

Pittsburgh was then a powerful town built on steel, oil, coal and gas. It was an industrial town that tried to redeem itself by spending lavishly on the arts.

At the time Cather was getting tired of toiling in the city's editorial and educational vineyards. She was not writing much fiction. Fortunately, Isabelle became her patron.

The two women were immediately attracted to each other and became lifelong friends. Isabelle insisted that Cather move into the stately home where her father, Judge Samuel McClung, and her mother, brother and sister, as well as a slew of servants, lived. Cather moved in as a temporary guest, but she ended up staying for many years and produced her first major works in the McClung mansion. Isabelle had had to use some emotional blackmail to get Cather accepted in the household. She told her parents she would leave if Cather couldn't live with them.

The family was socially prominent and entertained formally. Isabelle, however, was much more attracted to the company of artists and other bohemians than her fellow socialites.

Typically the two women would break away from the household after dinner and read Tolstoy, Turgenev and Balzac, among others, according to Cather biographer E.K Brown.

Isabelle's very conservative father was known for having given Alexander Berkman, the anarchist who shot and wounded industrialist Henry Clay Frick in 1892, the maximum sentence allowed -- 22 years, according to Eric Koch's *The Brothers Hambourg.*

Although Willa became increasingly politically conservative as she grew older she maintained a soft spot for Emma Goldman, the anarchist who was Berkman's lover and who was later deported to Russia. Cather met and became very fond of a young violinist who was a niece of Goldman, who was also a "socialist." Thus did the violinist David Hochstein became an heroic protagonist in some of her later writing.

Willa no doubt was circumspect about her opinions on the matter of Emma Goldman and Berkman at the McClung mansion, where Isabelle fixed up a sewing room on the third floor as a writer's study.

It was there that she began to craft the stories and novels that established her career. The two women also began to see the world together. In 1902, they sailed to England and then to France. Thus did Willa first head into the milieu that included the Menuhins. The vortex of it all occurred later in France -- a land Willa loved, although not without reservation.

Willa's third novel, *The Song of the Lark,* the story of the successful, striving artist Thea Kronberg, who comes from a small town on the plains, was published the same year Judge McClung died -- 1915.

By then, father and daughter had been Cather's patrons for more than a decade. When Willa had to move because the McClung house was being sold, it was a real wrench.

Her friendship with Isabelle never died, however. Whether it was a lifelong friendship or love affair can never be decisively proven.

It is said that Isabelle's marriage to Jan Hambourg, when she was forty and he was four years younger, was also a shock to Cather.

Nonetheless, Cather found the minister to perform "the Protestant-Jewish" wedding, according to Koch. She also arranged for the reception on April 3, 1916, at the Church of the Messiah in New York City.

Although Cather dedicated a couple of books to Hambourg, she also wrote about predatory Jewish men, one of whom resembled Hambourg. Hambourg was the model for Louis Marsellus, the grasping protagonist in *The Professor's House*, for example.

Later, however, she seemed to completely accept the marriage, growing to like Hambourg, who encouraged her to join the couple as often as possible, and she appreciated the fact that he seemed to make Isabelle happy. In a way, Isabelle and Jan were more than willing to continue playing the role of Cather's patrons. Hambourg was a thoroughly intelligent and charming man who loved Paris, music, books and food, perhaps in that order. The relationship of the three was obviously a pivotal and complex one. Cather stayed with the couple when they lived in New England where she wrote most of *My Antonia*. She later lived with them in Toronto. But by

1923, Isabelle and Jan had moved to Paris and then to Ville d'Avray, a suburb of Paris where various kinds of artists, including Willa, often stayed. But Cather found she could not work there even though the Hambourgs had prepared a study for her, hoping she would stay.

Willa does seem to have enjoyed herself thoroughly, however. While in Ville d'Avray, she met Eugène Ysaÿe, one of the world's greatest violinists who had been Hambourg's mentor and music teacher. There was much chamber music played at Ville d'Avray, and seven-year-old Yaltah had shined by climbing on the piano bench and playing Mozart with the others.

Hambourg was a good violinist, although not necessarily a great one. In any event, his wife's wealth made it unnecessary for him to pursue a career. He had made a specialty of studying the scores of Bach, and Yehudi, who played the solo Bach partitas quite beautifully throughout his career, regarded him as a serious scholar. He had also been a colleague of another great Bach scholar of the time, Albert Schweitzer.

The Menuhins had met the Hambourgs three years before they were to meet the Hambourgs' great friend and protegé, Willa Cather.

The Hambourgs lived in a luxury apartment on the Left Bank that had been built in 1728 by the banker of Louis XV. They also had an apartment in Ville d'Avray, where they lived with their parrot Coco.

Coco was apparently quite an amazing bird.

Koch quotes a composer who heard a violinist playing the opening bars of one of Bach's partitas at the Hambourg apartment.

The composer walked into the room.

"This I couldn't believe," the composer said. "I know

good fiddle playing when I hear it, and this was no parrot. However, Jan led me to a room containing a large birdcage, and in it sat an intelligent-looking, big, bright green parrot. It looked me over with a knowing, baleful eye, and Jan tried to coax it to -- I have to say to 'play' -- the Bach Prelude. But it wouldn't. We were leaving the room when I heard the same violinist 'play' the opening bars of Kreisler's Liebseslied. It was uncanny and it was Coco."

This same bird made an appearance in Cather's *Shadows on the Rock* published in 1931, except in her book the parrot is obviously an African Gray and not a "green parrot."

Willa's memory was probably more accurate than the composer's, because African Grays are peculiarly talented at music. (I have heard an African Gray who was quite a good improvisational jazz singer. My own African Gray used to sing what sounded for all the world like Hindemith, so appreciate and interesting were its harmonies.)

By the time Willa visited the Hambourgs during the summer of 1930, when she first met the Menuhins, she hadn't seen Isabelle for about seven years.

Willa told the Hambourgs she would love to stay with them, but felt that to write, it was better to be surrounded by the American landscape and idiom. Still, she was at least a partial Francophile (she had some ancestors from France) and she was also a student of French literature. It was not accidental that *Shadows on the Rock* took place in French Quèbec. So she fit right in, spending hours happily looking out on the Seine and not writing.

Willa's hours with the Hambourgs were not wasted because music was always a part of those times with them. On one such musical occasion, Willa commented on some medal the great violinist Eugène Ysaÿe was wearing, so he went to his room and brought back a sackful of medals and jewels he had gathered throughout his career.

He handed them to her, and Willa spent a considerable amount of time on the floor looking at each one of them.

Marutha had not been so amused by Ysaÿe. The Menuhins had come to Paris looking for a teacher and concerts for Yehudi in 1927. Paris was an important center of music in pre-World War II Europe, and it was certainly the place for them to go.

First there was a side trip to Brussels, however. Yehudi's first teacher, Louis Persinger, had insisted he first go to Ysaÿe, since Ysaÿe had been his own teacher. But Persinger hadn't taken into consideration the prudishness of the Menuhin parents.

Ysaÿe was willing to take Yehudi as a student -- although his main advice had been to study scales, since no teacher had ever made the prodigy do that -- but Marutha had been shocked by the master's mènage.

Ysaÿe's house in Brussels was on a lovely tree-lined street, but it also was in total disarray. Ysaÿe himself was in an advanced state of aging, and his young wife was very much in evidence. He was a weary man with hardly enough energy to lift his massive arms. But when Yehudi played Lalo's *Symphony Espagnole*, Ysaÿe sat up. Yes, he said, this was great playing. He was impressed and pleased that Yehudi was the student of one of his own students, Persinger.

He asked Yehudi to become a student, but Marutha said she would have to discuss the matter with Moshe back in Paris. Mother and son quickly left the depressing surroundings, resolving never to return again, or so the story goes.

It's also been suggested that the fact Mrs. Ysaÿe was in a negligee, had offended Marutha, who never went anywhere without her girdle.

Yehudi's European career had been dazzling. Yaltah recalled a particular scene in London where he was mobbed by fans after a concert, leaving her and Hephzibah terrified. Firefighters were dispatched to protect the family.

In the process, the Menuhins were becoming more European than American. Yaltah was soaking up French, this time not from books and teachers but in real conversations. Willa conceded that musicians had to go to Europe because that was where the great players, teachers, composers and audiences were. (She did not believe writers should settle in Europe -- a subject we will return to later.)

In 1931, Hambourg helped the Menuhins find a somewhat dilapidated but beautiful three-story villa not far from his. The house was rented from the Vian family, whose son Boris was an author who became known as a nightclub entertainer after the war.

Hambourg loaned the Menuhins his favorite cook and handyman to help run the place.

Among those who came to visit and make music with the newest family in residence were George Enesco, Pablo Casals, Jacques Thibaud and Pierre Monteux.

Yaltah was taking piano lessons from Joaquin Nin, Anais Nin's brother, who had studied with Alfred Cortot and later Marciel Ciampi, Enesco's accompanist. Yaltah also studied with Rudolph Serkin and in Rome with Armando Silvestri. It was Serkin who had taught Yaltah and Hephzibah, and who expressed the opinion that Yaltah was the most talented.

She was later to study with Carl Friedberg -- who had worked with Brahms, Myra Hess, Adolph Baller and Beveridge Webster.

It was Ciampi who had immortalized Marutha when she insisted he hear Hephzibah, who had already had three years of piano instruction in San Francisco by the time she was seven years of age. After Hephzibah played, Yaltah, then five, played with equal prodigiousness, according to Humphrey Burton's *Menuhin: A Life*.

Ciampi heard the two girls and then said "Madame Menuhin's womb is a veritable conservatoire." He became their teacher.

Ville d'Avray was also home to people such as Edmond Rostand Jr., son of the author of *Cyrano de Bergerac*. The town had had a reputation as an artist's center for some time.

According to Burton, summer Sunday afternoons at the Menuhin home were usually devoted to marathon chamber music sessions. At one of these, Cortot, Thibaud and Casals were playing. Then Cortot on a second piano accompanied Hephzibah in the Schumann Piano Concerto. On that occasion, Marutha remarked that she didn't want Hephzibah to become a professional musician.

Nine-year-old Yaltah joined in with some Mozart.

Burton describes another incident when Yaltah was 12, and Moshe called her "the devil in the family." She insisted on going to see "Little Women" in a Paris cinema, the second film they had seen in 18 months.

(Years later, however, I had to sneak out myself to see Sunday matinees because my mother was so anxious to "protect" me from Hollywood "junk.")

There was no way that the Menuhin family could have stayed in France, of course, as the clouds of World War II and the Holocaust were gathering.

America beckoned, because it was home, after all. Shortly after first meeting Willa in France in 1930, the Menuhins made Manhattan their home base. This was where Yaltah and Hephzibah got to know Willa. And Willa had a thorough indoctrination in mind -- she wanted the children to under-stand the value of American culture.

CHAPTER EIGHT
Willa & Marutha

As World War II approached, the Menuhins head-quartered themselves in Manhattan where Willa was living.

Willa started seeing the Menuhin family frequently in New York early in the 1930s, which was made possible by the fact that Marutha and Willa so quickly bonded with each other. The connection the two women had was surprising considering that Willa had previously written about musical prodigies as if they were circus freaks.

But Willa thoroughly approved of what the Menuhin parents were doing and found the children a bright spot in her declining years. The fact that the children were not allowed to bask in the glow of the public adulation that surrounded them, that they lived disciplined, indeed overly disciplined lives, strongly appealed to her.

After a concert, the children ate and went to bed. Nothing special. Just another day in the life of a child!

Part of the reason may have been that Willa and Marutha both put great emphasis on adherence to one's principles at all costs. They both had strict value systems -- although Marutha's code may have been more arbitrary and certainly more irrational than Willa's.

Of course Willa must have had a blind spot when it came

to the miserable way Marutha, in particular, treated Yaltah. Even so, however, she appeared to have instinctively known of it, for she doted on Yaltah even more than the other children -- and more than that, she tried to teach Yaltah to be disciplined about whatever future travails life would present.

Did she see Yaltah as an abused child? If she did, she gave no direct indication of this. But she must have known something was wrong.

According to Edith Lewis, Willa's lifelong companion, the children "were not only the most gifted children Willa Cather had ever known, with that wonderful aura of imaginative charm, prescience, inspiration, that even the most gifted lose after they grow up; they were also extremely lovable, affectionate, and unspoiled; in some ways funnily naive, in others sensitive and discerning far beyond their years."

Cather would have gladly left any other chapter out of her life but the time she spent with the Menuhin children, Edith Lewis proclaimed.

Marutha's efforts to keep all unnecessary distractions out of the lives of her children particularly appealed to Willa, because her craft also thrived on solitude and on unbroken concentration. Willa had the same trouble any writer experienced. She had to gather the threads of a story's narrative from the ether before they eluded her. Writers -- or musician concentrating on a new work -- all understand the damage that even a good friend's well-intentioned phone call can do at the wrong moment.

From her letters and writing, it was obvious that Willa got a lot of her connection to creativity from being around music -- even the atmosphere of music. Indeed, she was one of those people who need music. On a few occasions, it seemed as if she enjoyed being in public, but mostly she did not.

Still, she understood that musical performers have to conduct their art in public. She, of course, only had to appear in public after the sacred act of writing was completed.

Edith Lewis shared Cather's feeling about the Menuhin children, and she helped Cather keep a scrapbook of photos mixed with newspaper stories and critical reviews, according to Phyllis C. Robinson's 1983 study, *Willa: The Life of Willa Cather*.

Interestingly enough, Yaltah always referred to Lewis by her full name -- Edith Lewis, whereas Willa was often just Willa and on more formal references, "Aunt Willa."

Lewis noted that the children regarded Willa as their greatest hero.

And it was a two way street.

Cather's friend Elizabeth Shepley Sergeant wrote in *Willa Cather: A Memoir*, that "Yehudi for Willa opened vistas into the world of the masters of music to which her own passion had never led.

"She made a story of this prodigy and his fascinating and gifted little sisters, and of his parents, as if she had at last, by proxy, a family exactly to her taste. Not at all like her beloved father's family with its pioneer tradition; in this brilliant Jewish milieu, erudition and art were primary, and everything else of secondary importance."

It was rare for Marutha and Moshe to endorse anyone wholeheartedly as a teacher, but they approved of Aunt Willa. Marutha trusted her with her children explicitly.

There is almost no other person who was allowed to take the three children out -- as Willa did when she would take them for a walk in Central Park, to talk about philosophy, religion, art and life.

Marutha wanted to keep her children out of public view,

so they would begin their walks through Central Park at 6 a.m.

During that time, Willa became not only a teacher of literature and philosophy, but developed into a kind of moral authority as well, ready to give romantic advice.

Some years later, Willa became Yehudi's confidant in romantic matters. For example, she made it plain that she felt Yehudi would be best off marrying a woman like his mother.

Yehudi had asked Aunt Willa about the sadness he felt upon a perceived failed relationship. Her reply: "A little heartache is a good companion for a young man on his holiday."

The great novelist was loyal to Marutha to a fault. She advised Yehudi that American women were frivolous. "I rather think you will need a girl with a more disciplined nature than our girls are likely to have." Her advice to Yehudi: marry a woman like your mother, "slight, heroic, delicate, unconquerable."

And to a considerable extent, that's just what he did in his second marriage.

Nola -- his first wife -- was not at all like Marutha. Diana, Yehudi's second wife, had many more elements of his mother.

In any event, when his marriage to Nola was breaking up, he spoke to Willa about it. It is not known exactly what was said.

If Willa had not been a woman of great integrity, one might have suspected she was conniving with Marutha. But she no doubt meant what she said about Marutha, who from Yaltah's perspective was a mean and evil woman. Curiously, Marutha kept a shelf full of voodoo dolls and Yaltah would never shake the belief that she was one of the victims of her mother's evil works. Everyone from recalcitrant relatives to failed instructors of the children were banished to the cauldrons of hell, and seldom resurrected depending on Marutha's emotional state.

But the bond between Marutha and Willa seemed never to slacken. It burned brightly with a fixed focus; there appeared to never be a separation between them.

Yet their thoughts were diametrically opposed. In Marutha's world, women did not pursue concert careers. Her daughters were to stay at home and raise their own children. After all, that's what Marutha, who had originally taught cello and piano in Jerusalem, did.

Marutha remained as strong in these sentiments throughout her life as Willa did in her beliefs. Early on Willa had told a friend that "nothing mattered ... but writing books, and living the kind of life that made it possible to write them."

Willa believed that a great career and marriage could not co-exist for a woman. In fact she had always felt very intensely, from childhood that to accomplish anything noteworthy, one had to be a man.

As a child Willa called herself William Cather -- in fact she signed herself sometimes as William Cather Jr. or William Cather M.D. Because she so admired the doctor who had helped her combat an illness, she thought she would one day study medicine. Willa got some practical doctoring experience when she worked as his assistant.

Willa was to keep her tomboy ways until she left Red Cloud. By the time she left Red Cloud and was beginning to make her mark as a music and drama critic, newspaperwoman, teacher and most of all writer, she sometimes dressed quite femininely.

It is not that Marutha was romantic about marriage. Probably Willa had a lot more romanticism than did Marutha. To Marutha, marriage was a barnyard matter with no room for romance. When she told Yaltah that "I picked a good father for you," her tone was devoid of humor.

In Marutha's view it was simple: you mated with the most appropriate person for your class and economic position, and it didn't really matter if you loved him or not. She expressed about the same attitude toward her children and grandchildren's bowel movements. She had no respect for privacy in areas where she considered her snooping important.

Willa probably would not have been that kind of a mother had she had children, although having children was not a concern of hers. She was dedicated to her writing. Still, she wrote well about women who had children -- such as in *My Antonia*.

One of the most famous quotes from a Willa Cather work is from Thea in *The Song of the Lark*, who offhandedly remarks "who marries who is a small matter." That must have resonated with Marutha tremendously.

There were many letters between Marutha and Willa, and they no doubt would have been interesting to read. But in accordance with Willa's wishes, Marutha burned all of her letters when Cather died.

My mother early on must have rejected Marutha's notion of what a woman is and should be. I think it was in part because she learned a different role model from Willa's women. Surely Yaltah understood relatively early, as she began rejecting her mother's notions, that Cather's fictional women were aspects of Aunt Willa herself.

The bond between Marutha and Willa was, like both women, enigmatic. Perhaps what they shared was as simple as the fact that, in the world in which they had been born, women and their biological role, were somewhat akin to farm animals, just as men were "beasts of burden" who often died young from doing hard, dangerous work.

Certainly Cather's characters Thea, Lucy and Antonia are

not romantics. Neither was their creator. The relationships of men and women in Cather's writing are strong and real and good and bad. They are never schmaltzy.

While Yaltah and Yehudi and Hephzibah had abiding respect for Cather, Yaltah later said, "My father worshipped Marutha and he wanted us to worship her. And we tried. It comes very naturally to worship people when you're young ... but one should have a chance to select the object of one's worship."

Yaltah went on to say that it is possible to learn a new religion, and perhaps one should have been willing to join the cult of Marutha, "but alas we never did."

She continued: "If we had been tougher children, we probably would have said, 'That's enough of that.' And we might have stopped it. As it was, we even took the San Francisco fog seriously, for instance. We really thought the fog was part of God's plan for us, and so we had to bear it. And so we resorted to inner vision. We had our dream world, which was wonderful. It's still very hard to get out of that dream world. And in times of trouble, that's the world one goes into, the inner world. Because the outer world is collapsing."

Yaltah said that her mother remained an enigma to the end of her long life. Psychologically Marutha dwelled all her life in isolation. This resulted in "a terrible unfeeling coldness."

Yaltah added that studies had been made of children who were raised as the Menuhins were, without real love and in a controlling environment. She said that while the parents made sure that every single moment was programmed -- you took a book when you went for a walk in the park -- they also made sure the children had no privacy.

Even as teenagers, personal mail was supposed to be opened at the dinner table and discussed.

"Of course children love to have some private area, or some relationship, all their own," my mother told filmmaker Tony Palmer. "But in our case, all our letters had to be read aloud to each other before we were allowed to eat. They were mostly letters from teachers or relations, mostly quite superficial letters in fact. They certainly weren't romantic letters. Mother never had to check our virtue."

Yaltah felt that her mother "was sitting on a tremendous amount of resentment" toward her husband which she took out on her daughter because of the physical resemblance father and daughter shared.

"Childhood is such a short time that we should have been allowed to take advantage of it. We never realized the stupidity of many grown ups, for instance, because [as children] we began to take everything so seriously. Still, at least we can now be children for the rest of our lives; that's what Yehudi told Hephzibah and me. Certainly we never knew, until it was much too late, how utterly isolated we were, that we were not living the life of children at all."

Later in life, Yaltah expressed her bitterness at the fact that her mother had allowed her and her sister to practice and play music but did not conceive of either of them following a career.

No, it was "just to get the birds to come." Piano playing was an enticement in attracting a husband, because soon the girls were supposed to have lots of children, Yaltah said.

"We weren't even told how that happened. So Hephzibah and I had a very romantic understanding of life with no understanding of human beings, our own selves included," she said.

She went on to explain that "Mother was quite indifferent to whether a husband loved his wife or a wife loved her husband. The question was did he have money and did he come from a well-to-do family? These were the great moral and philosophical questions for her."

Yaltah felt that she and her sister were like children being led to the slaughter.

Thus, for Yaltah, being able to talk to Willa about a story she was writing was magical. Willa offered a set of values entirely different from those of Marutha.

Perhaps Marutha didn't realize how profoundly subversive to her intent Cather could be, especially with Yaltah and Hephzibah. Yaltah said that her father was intensely fascinated by *Lucy Gayheart*, because of the enigmatic suggestion that Lucy had died not just by accident but by suicide.

On the surface, Lucy would never have committed suicide -- she was too strong a life force, which is what made her such a great literary figure. The slippery part comes from the fact that Cather made it plain in her letters and writing that she had ambivalent feelings about Lucy -- maybe that's why her death was inevitable.

Sometimes Lucy's character got on Willa's nerves tremendously, and at one point she told a friend she regarded Lucy as "silly."

Yaltah no doubt talked to her about Lucy all the time, and Willa apparently said enough to Moshe as well to convince him that Lucy committed suicide and did not just drown in an unfortunate accident.

Yaltah pointed out that Moshe was obsessed with suicide because his favorite sister, Shandel, committed suicide on the eve of her arranged marriage to an older man she did not love.

It appeared that when Cather contemplated the inevitability of Lucy's death by answering Moshe's questions about her, she was being much more explicit than she ever was in her own novel.

It is not an accident that in *Lucy Gayheart*, Lucy leaves behind three fleeing footsteps cast in concrete for posterity -- literally.

Harry Gordon, Lucy's spurned lover, had been there when as a child Lucy made the impressions in freshly-poured concrete while trying to jump across the concrete steps. As Lucy jumped, she looked straight at Harry, who was crouching nearby. As she fled, she begged him not to tell anyone what had just happened. That, as it turned out, was his first encounter with her. It was the moment that bound their lives together forever. Only Harry knew where the footsteps had come from.

After Lucy's death, Gordon walks out to the Lucy Gayheart house, which was still there on the furthermost pavement at the edge of town.

Gordon, who is also arguably the man responsible for Lucy's death, looks again at her footprints and treasures them the rest of his life. He sees in them Lucy's swiftness, mischief and lightness. He ponders whether the footsteps look as if they were made by someone running away, or whether they just look that way to him because he was there when Lucy ran by.

In any event, these were certainly the qualities conjured up by the patter of the Menuhin children's feet as Willa wrote *Lucy Gayheart*.

I know that swiftness, lightness and mischief and are apt descriptions of my mother, whose life force I'm sure Willa borrowed as she created Lucy.

★

Marutha was no doubt convinced by Willa's compelling arguments that the children would suffer if they had only a smattering of many languages, which was the effect of Marutha's educational goals for them.

The children early on studied classical literature in French, Italian, German and Russian, which pleased Marutha. But Cather pointed out that her children were American, and their native language was English -- or better yet American.

They needed to be grounded and have a sense of place -- this was necessary for any artist, Cather argued.

Marutha agreed that Cather should become the children's Shakespeare teacher.

The lessons started with *Richard II* and then moved on to *Macbeth* and *Henry IV*. The lessons were so popular that Yehudi soon insisted on joining them. He didn't want to be left out of the fun.

E.K. Brown's classic *Willa Cather: A Critical Biography*, published by Knopf in 1953, noted that the Menuhins affected Cather's own writing.

She loved to get Temple Editions of Shakespeare for her sessions with the children. Brown wrote, "In *Lucy Gayheart*, there is a reminiscence of these sessions and of the Temple Shakespeare." He points to a scene where Clement Sebastian, the great singer Lucy falls in love with, "runs his finger along a row of small red leather volumes, and pulls one out of its place."

Lucy mistakenly thinks the play "a rather foolish comedy where everybody was pretending, and nobody was in earnest."

It wasn't until she began to accompany Sebastian singing a song from Shakespeare's "Twelfth Night" that she realized "she had never known that words had any value aside from their direct meaning."

Yehudi said that Willa "admired what she felt had not been her birthright -- the old, the European, the multilayered, and above all, music."

When he asked her what she thought about his staying

in Europe, she said: "If we remain always in our land we miss the companionship of seasoned and disciplined minds. Here there are no standards of taste and no response to art except emotional ones."

Having said all this, she added "if we adopt Europe altogether, we lose that sense of belonging which is so important, and we lose part of our reality."

And as part of her concern that Yaltah was too influenced by the French language, she told my mother that a writer especially can't stop being American and become French, no matter how much he would like to.

To illustrate, Willa told Yaltah the story of a talented American writer who got so fed up with his own country he went to France. He dissipated his talent because he did not write about the country he came from. He persisted in writing about France, and he could not compete with French writers writing about their own land in their own language.

Willa was not only the children's mentor -- especially Yaltah's -- she was their playmate. She would go sledding in the snow in Central Park with them, and Yehudi would afterwards store the sled in her apartment.

Yaltah, however, appeared to be her absolute favorite. Sometimes she took Yaltah to see Shakespeare plays, to walk in the park, to the opera, or perhaps to visit a museum or an art gallery.

In the spring of 1933, Cather was giving twice-weekly Shakespeare lessons to the Menuhins, and spending odd hours trolling bookstores for Shakespeare for the children to read from.

Edith Lewis was usually in attendance, and all would take turns reading parts of Shakespeare. Then Willa would comment

on the language and the situations the characters found themselves in.

The Menuhins lived off Central Park. Cather's apartment
was at 63rd Street and Park Avenue, so in addition to the
Shakespeare there were also plenty of walks and outings.

Lewis said that Cather loved the family as a whole and each
separate member individually.

They had been raised by a stern taskmistress who marched
to her own tune and drumbeat, and Cather admired the way
Marutha worked to keep the children unaware of the public impression they were making. Willa admired the fact that
Marutha made her children dress plainly.

But Willa herself liked to sometimes dress colorfully and
even outlandishly, and Yaltah later in life loved wearing colorful clothes. Indeed, in her last years, colorful clothes were
almost a trademark by which people recognized Yaltah walking down the street.

It probably was no accident that Hephzibah once told Willa
that "To me, a woman without jewels is not a woman."

Lewis said that the years of the Menuhin family visits to
New York were like a "continuous festival, full of concerts
and gay parties." The Cather apartment was decorated with
flowers and small orange trees. Their luncheons invariably
included caviar and champagne. Then there were trips to the
opera, long walks around the reservoir in Central Park and
most importantly, discussions about art, religion, philosophy
and life.

In *Willa: The Life of Willa Cather*, Phyllis C. Robinson reported that almost daily Willa would stop by and see if the children wanted to join her walking around the reservoir.

Sometimes a note would be hand delivered to her "dar-
lingest Yaltah," for whom she had developed a particular

fondness, asking her if she wanted to go for a walk.

Sometimes, said Robinson, a pressed autumn leaf would be delivered by a "carrier pigeon," who carried Willa's love along on its wings.

When the children were on tour, as often they were, Willa looked forward with great expectations to their long letters about their experiences.

Willa was struck by a terrible melancholy while working on *Lucy Gayheart*, that took hold of her after her parents' death and her last trip to Red Cloud. She was in her 70s when she began writing *Lucy*.

It didn't help that the country was in the clutches of the Great Depression, and many in her family and some of her most beloved friends were broke and ill, including Isabelle. She did what she could to help them, but all this took its toll.

As she began writing *Lucy*, she also had physical problems. She sprained the big tendon in her left wrist, ignoring the pain until it became unbearable. With her hand in a splint, and infection setting in, she found it impossible to write.

She got through this bleak period by attending many of Yehudi's concerts and spending days on end with the Menuhins.

Even if she had not been having so much trouble writing *Lucy*, Edith Lewis says that she would have made time for the Menuhins. "They discussed very abstract subjects together -- art, religion, philosophy, life. If Willa Cather had been writing *War and Peace*, I am sure she would have abandoned it to take these walks," Lewis said.

The children felt that too. "I remember feeling awfully loved and safe in her presence," Hephzibah said. She noted that in those years, Cather may have been feeling bleak and depressed but she was never crabby around the children.

There was no piano in Cather's apartment; they went there to talk of literature, people, events and the books she was writing. She came to the Menuhins' hotel -- usually the Ansonia (on the West Side, a favorite of European opera singers) -- and they all sat around a table and read aloud the different parts of Hamlet.

Willa was carried away by the beauty of the language and the message of the play, and she shared these strong emotions with the children. She was never dry or academic, Yehudi remembered.

Many years later in London, Yaltah laughed at an old post-card that fell out of a book in her flat. It was from Edith Lewis, who used to attend those Ansonia sessions. "You saw the things she saw," Lewis gushed. But Yaltah felt that Cather went far beyond that. She somehow enveloped the reader in the truest world of the artist. She said that Willa never insisted that they look at things her way, but it was "her absorption and her concentration that was so contagious."

"I wish we had known her when we were older," Yaltah said. "But then she might not have been so open with us."

For Yaltah
Another reminder of my
affectionate thoughts
Myra

Yaltah was never sure what she thought of the great pianist Myra Hess, who was a good friend of Willa Cather and a teacher of Yaltah.

CHAPTER NINE

Secrets Willa Told Yaltah

illa and Yaltah talked a lot about language when they got together or whenever Willa wrote to her.

Cather praised good English prose over French, which she tended to dismiss as "extravagant, vague and flowery." English, she said, should be plain and simple without a lot of "drawn-out sighs."

It was not that she didn't have respect for the French. She allowed that the older French prose was "less flowery and frivolous and more deep running, like the English."

Some of Willa's chatty letters to Yaltah would digress from literature and philosophy to talking about Myra Hess who had come for tea yesterday, and sent you "love and love and love."

Myra Hess was the famous pianist who was Yaltah's teacher for a while. In some ways the two older women were very alike, both quite strong and mannish in appearance. But from various comments about Hess, it was apparent Yaltah did not love her the way she loved Willa.

Hess -- who incidentally was one of the great defenders of *Lucy Gayheart* -- was a great pianist, and I know that Yaltah felt she learned a lot musically from her, but Yaltah also felt Hess was too strong, arbitrary and demanding. Oddly, Yaltah's third husband, Joel Ryce, had also studied under Hess.

My mom noted that not all great artists were great company like Aunt Willa. Hess was an exacting and demanding teacher who wanted to control the environment around her.

In a way Hess was a bit like the composer Ernst Bloch -- very problematical as a human being, Yaltah said. Yaltah greatly admired and beautifully performed and loved the music of the great Jewish Swiss composer. But she remembers that in person, especially if you saw too much of him on a regular basis, he was also a kind of divine malcontent, and sometimes when the children saw him coming, they'd run.

This was never the case with Cather.

Cather was not a tyrant about her views. But she had a great power to imbue Yaltah with a strong sense of philosophical idealism. She talked to Yaltah of the nature of things in no uncertain terms. She spoke from a deeply religious nature. She was a committed dualist -- for her, the material and the spiritual existed on two distinct plains.

Yaltah was an apt student. Willa taught her that the key to understanding is imagination. In a letter to Yaltah, Cather spoke about how we can't see the shadow of even material things with our physical eyes; more important, she said, are the eyes of the soul, whether they are found in the brain, heart or nerves.

Cather used the word "quiver" to describe what must happen inside one before the eyes can really "see." She said that she hoped Yaltah recovered from a cold and when she saw her in a few weeks, she hoped she would be as plump as ever.

★

Cold predominates in Willa's writings -- such as when in *My Antonia*, Antonia's family arrives from Bohemia and faces living on the raw prairie. They have no farmhouse, only a small, primitive dwelling in a rock cave during the dead of winter. Knowing this, the descriptions of cold when Willa writes to the young girl Yaltah become more important.

Yet somehow Antonia's family survived -- and from the powerful way Willa described the harsh climate and the toll it took, you knew that she had also experienced the cold as a child on the plains.

There is much commentary in Willa's letters of the rain and the snow, sunshine and warmth. She said the harshest weather was invigorating, even when it was leaden and gloomy.

She described one New York winter as "bitter," producing a freezing wind that cuts the face.

So her sympathy was genuine when Moshe told her that Yaltah had horrid bronchitis, but she offered Yaltah an alternative view.

She told Yaltah to be glad she was in a warm place, which is the basic thing you need to get over such an illness. Cather said this with all the assurance of the doctor she had once vowed to become.

In her letters to Yaltah, Cather went from philosophy and literature to weather and health in an instant, because they were one and the same to her.

She particularly noted that nothing makes one feel more miserable than having breathing problems.

But she added that in not too long a time the heavy feeling in Yaltah's chest would disappear and life would come rushing back.

Cather told Yaltah she knew that awful choking feeling because it was a nightly struggle for her when she was laid low by influenza.

A number of times Willa told Yaltah how much pleasure Yehudi's gift of a miniature orange tree had given her. The orange tree also produced wonderfully sweet juice.

Not all was sweetness and light in Willa's discussions, however, just as it is not in her writing.

She suggests that Yaltah read a story of hers about a rat. Willa said as a child she had a twelve-pound rat she loved devotedly. He was a hunter, and he killed his prey.

It was in the nature of things. Some of the best writing in *My Antonia* comes when a young boy saves Antonia -- or at least she believes he has -- by apparently killing a huge rattlesnake that had cornered them. That the huge old rattlesnake might have already been dead is only suggested as a possibility.

★

Another trait that Yaltah and Willa shared was a religious nature. Of the three Menuhins, Yaltah was easily the most religious. This may have helped create a special bond between Yaltah and Willa.

Willa, for example, often talked to Yaltah about the Bible as literature.

She described a play by J.M. Barrie (author of *Peter Pan*), "The Boy David," and told Yaltah she would send her the book, which she obviously admired. It hadn't done well in London, she said, because hardly anyone there read the Old Testament.

Particularly good was how Barrie showed the manner in which the the future man was in the boy, she said.

Willa conceded that Barrie was a bit sentimental, but thought he could get away with it because he had an ability to laugh at himself.

Cather told Yaltah that no one on earth could write poetry as beautiful as the Psalms of David.

In one letter Willa commented on the Menuhin's plan to retire from the public for "Mother's Year" in 1936. During that period Yehudi would not perform in public, but would stay at home in California with his parents and sisters.

Willa said the time in California would either make them so homesick for Paris they would have to return, or that perhaps in ten years they would be intensely glad that they had a place in California to retire to.

She recommended being alone -- with no books, no music, only the stars and the elements. The poetry Yaltah wrote a bit later suggests she took that to heart. As children are prone to do, Yaltah did a lot of communing alone with the spectacular night sky in Los Gatos.

Aunt Willa was not the best person to talk to about current political issues, however. Yaltah asked Aunt Willa in a letter about the fascist conquest and destruction of the Spanish Republic, and her only response was that Spain was "going mad."

I take this educated leap because Cather replied to one of Yaltah's letters about going to South Africa and visiting the diamond mines, by saying that she preferred to be on top of the earth instead of under the ground. This rather flip answer sidestepped the obvious real questions the young girl was posing.

I know that my mother saw the gaunt faces of miners in South Africa when she accompanied Yehudi on a tour there. The memory was seared into her consciousness, for she talked about it all the years I was growing up.

The diamond mines belonged to the Oppenheim family, who were hosting Yehudi and his family. The trip into a mine was merely part of the visit, but the images stayed with my mother in a most intense and personal way. I think she was able to glimpse from the visit what it would be like to lack a privileged upbringing, to have to work all one's life in a confined, dark, dangerous environment.

The children sent Aunt Willa books, and she sent them books. At one point she sent Yaltah a book and admonished her to perk up, that she no longer had to pretend she had forgotten that particular book Willa, which had promised her.

Stressing the importance of keeping her promise, Willa inscribed the book to Yaltah and Hephzibah, but unfortunately it was a wet sticky day and she made a mess of the inscription. Still, she sent it.

Willa was always telling the children how much she loved them, and it rings as absolutely authentic. She said she wished she could give them a hug as strong as Russian bears. Noting the weather had been wonderful and cold with lots of snow, Cather said she missed the children as walking partners.

Even her notes to Yaltah to meet her for a walk at the 48th Street entrance to the Menuhins' hotel had a pleading quality. She asked almost plaintively where she might hope for an hour with her, and even said she would wait a bit for Yaltah if she couldn't get down promptly by noon. Meanwhile, she was also complaining that most of her effort at that time was going to stop a French publisher from bringing out a poorly translated edition of *Death Comes for the Archbishop*.

Once when the Menuhin phone was turned off for a couple of days, Cather sent a letter saying she had been trying to call. She also observed what a lot of creative people have no doubt felt, that phones should normally be shut off except to talk to the butcher and the grocer. But in this case, she realized how much she missed talking to the Menuhins. Marutha was quite ill, and no calls were coming in or out of the Menuhin compound.

In 1938 when Yaltah accompanied Yehudi in a recording of the Mozart Sonata in B Flat Major, Cather told Yaltah she had played it on the record player many times. It was almost as good as an actual visit, Cather said.

That recording was played at Yaltah's funeral in London in June of 2001.

★

I personally treasure one of Cather's rare typewritten letters, dated 1944. In that letter she congratulated Yaltah on her music making. She said that -- amazingly -- Marutha had bragged about her daughter playing concerts "long enough and big enough for a young giant."

And she also noticed that Lionel at 17 months of age was no longer a baby but a boy!

I saw that from birth I was surrounded by magic and music. I realized how truly I had been under the spell of music from the start. In the first year of my birth, I was hearing music. My mother would put me in a baby basket under the piano. Thus I always thought of thundering, glorious melodies coming from a heavenly keyboard just above me.

My first memory of Willa was hearing my mother read aloud that letter. Even years later, I hadn't realized the tremendous effect Willa had had on me, just because I was my mother's son.

CHAPTER TEN
When Only The Night Sky Counts

Yehudi and Hephzibah had been performing together in Europe, but upon their return to American
soil, Moshe stuck to the party line when mention was made
of Hephzibah. Yaltah was not even an issue, despite the high
praise for her playing.

"Hephzibah could have a quality music career but not a
quantity one. We are modern and radical. The world is not radical enough for us," Moshe said, and then explained, apparently without any sense of irony, that "the first urge of a woman
is to have a home."

Yaltah's hopes for a career didn't have a chance.

During "Mother's Year," which began in 1936, the
Menuhins moved into what had once been a priest's dwelling
on the Jesuit novitiate atop the highest hill in Los Gatos. Yehudi
was turning 20 and the idea was that the family would with-
draw from public view for the transition to adulthood.
Carefully screened young men and women were sometimes
allowed to visit; the Menuhins put on plays -- Yehudi was
Cyrano in Rostand's "Cyrano de Bergerac" -- the same
Rostand family they knew in Ville d'Avray. Hephzibah was
Roxanne and Yaltah was "everyone else."

When during a rare public interview during "Mother's

Year," Yaltah voiced the thought that their California home was "very pleasant" but that she missed her friends in Paris, Marutha interjected: "She yearns for Europe and solo recitals and a career of her own. I say that it is better she should be happy than famous."

No doubt foremost in Yaltah's mind among their "European friends" was Willa, for she had met Aunt Willa in Paris.

The Menuhins settled in Los Gatos because in 1934 Yehudi had purchased a five-square-mile piece of land, nearby in the Santa Cruz Mountains. A grand house was supposed to be built there. The idea was that this estate, called Alma, would become the home for generations of Menuhins. A more realistic mansion, Villa Cherkess, was finally built, but was almost never lived in.

Los Gatos is about 50 miles from San Francisco and 20 miles from Santa Cruz, just up the road from Salinas and Carmel. This was and partially remains God's country, celebrated by the poet Robinson Jeffers, by Henry Miller, Jack Kerouac, and others. The Menuhins spent some time at Alma, but mostly remained on a couple of different pieces of property in town -- one was the five-acre Rancho Yaltah. Later, they moved to a much smaller place next to the Novitiate, the last home of Moshe and Marutha.

The Menuhins had been directed toward Los Gatos by George Dennison and Frank Ingerson in Paris, during a visit at the Hambourgs'. The "boys," as they were called, were in Paris because of their San Francisco patron, Cora Koshland.

The "boys" owned Cathedral Oaks, on which the two gay portrait painters and society artists collected hundreds of cats, most of whom lived outside. The artists lived in a nine-room, high-ceilinged redwood house built in 1925.

The most famous art work by "the boys" was their reproduction of the Ark of the Covenant at Temple Emanu-El in San Francisco. It was built in London, took 14 months to complete, stood 10 feet tall and weighed 3,000 pounds. It was covered with thin hammered gold, old cedar and jewel-covered enameling. It had a Torah, containing the book of Moses, inside.

The sculptured enamels of ancient times were carefully reconstituted by the artists who were emulating a process that had not been used since the early Greeks.

Ingerson and Dennison also created the Coconut Grove night club at the Ambassador Hotel in Los Angeles. This famous club was crowded nightly with stars during the golden age of Hollywood in the 1930s and early 1940s.

Oddly enough, the Lockheed Missile and Space Corporation was born at Alma. The land was originally part of a ranch owned by Flora Raines Loughead, and her sons, Malcolm and Allan, used a barn to build early automobiles and aircraft.

Alma became home to the Alma Trio, which included Yehudi's accompanist George Baller, cellist Gabor Rejto and various violinists when they came through on tour.

Years later, Rejto and Yaltah were musical touring partners.

Hephzibah and Yaltah fell in love with two brothers who frequented Los Gatos during "Mother's Year" -- Daniel and Maurice Fleg.

Yaltah said Marutha was so afraid of the budding romance between Hephzibah and Maurice Fleg, that she destroyed a letter Fleg had written to Hephzibah proposing marriage. Marutha didn't want her eldest daughter thrown off-course. She wanted to make a better match for her eldest daughter than a relatively poor Jewish artist. Maurice was the son of

Edmond Fleg, a French Jewish writer and a Zionist, who had written librettos with Enesco.

At the same time, the man young Yaltah really loved was Daniel Fleg, Maurice's brother. Yaltah wrote love poems to him in French, English and Italian. He had been allowed to join in the swimming, walking and music that were part of "Mother's Year." But Marutha soon banished him from the inner circle as well.

Daniel and Yaltah never kissed, because Marutha never left them alone. Yaltah told me he went back to Paris and drowned himself in the Seine in 1941, shortly after his brother had died at Auschwitz. Yaltah said he was disconsolate about his brother, but he was equally upset for having been excommunicated from the Menuhin court.

Marutha tried to get rid of her youngest daughter first in the serious matchmaking that began in "Mother's Year."

Yaltah had been offered as a consolation prize to one of Hephzibah's suitors. William Stix was rich, so Marutha thought it might be a good enough marriage for Yaltah, whether she wanted him or not.

Willa was present in New York on June 7, 1938, when Yaltah was married off. Willa wrote that she couldn't help but steal glances at the beautiful bride, so dazzling was she.

Cather must have seen how frightened Yaltah was -- certainly her sister did. The real story may be in how Willa appeared so oblivious to the mother's treatment of her younger daughter. Sue Rosowski, a prominent Cather scholar at the University of Nebraska, told me she too had pondered Willa's blind spot to Marutha's treatment of Yaltah and found no real answers.

Since the grand design was right, Willa must have felt the details were grand as well. Cather perhaps over-appreciated how Marutha proudly marched to the beat of her own drum -- and believed that therefore, Marutha was basically doing the right things by her children's talents.

Maybe Willa even considered that in the scheme of things, Yaltah was not so badly treated. How about all the children left without homes and parents because of war and famine? Perhaps Willa saw Marutha was an incredibly unfeeling character, but her cruelties were confined to words and sometimes voodoo, when needed. At least she didn't physically beat her daughter.

In any event, Yaltah later recalled a conversation she had with her father on the eve of her marriage to William Stix in 1938.

"I'd had marvelous conversations with my father. And I remember him telling me one day about the sister he loved very dearly who had killed herself. It seems that she too had been sent a letter from another man, who was her real true love, the night before her intended marriage to someone else. Believing that her true love had forsaken her -- the letter having been intercepted by an older sister who was really like a mother to her -- and not being able to face a loveless marriage, she poisoned herself. And my father's eyes were so full of pain when he told me this. And he'd tell it like a secret, so that no one should be let in on the burden he felt he was carrying. He said that, if only he had known, he could have saved her. And when did he choose to tell me this? In 1938, when I was about to be married to a man he knew I didn't love."

Yaltah remembered her mother dressed in black for her wedding to Stix. Hephzibah remembered waving goodbye to Yaltah at Grand Central Station as she rushed off to begin married life, carrying a battered school briefcase with some of her favorite musical scores, volumes of French poetry and a notebook of her childhood verse. She cried and looked pathetic, her sister recalled.

Stix, who was a St. Louis department store heir, also worked as an attorney for the Senate Civil Liberties Committee. After the New York wedding, the young couple moved to Washington D.C. Six months later she was back in Los Gatos. Her marriage was annulled because it was never consummated, and her father was telling reporters that his daughter was "completely immature."

He later declared, "Yaltah married the wrong man. She was only sixteen but she made a mistake."

Later Bill Koshland who became president of Alfred A. Knopf, fell in love with Yaltah and maybe also with her poetry. He read much of it and encouraged her.

Koshland went to work for Alfred and Blanche Knopf in 1934 and in 1966 succeeded Blanche as president of the publishing company. He was Cather's editor in the '30s and '40s.

Koshland told me of his relationship with my mother, but did not go into details.

After Yaltah returned from her failed marriage in St. Louis, Marutha became worse.

There was a possible relationship developing between Yaltah and Keith Pulvermacher, whose father was the editor of London's *Daily Telegraph*. Marutha told the elder Pulvermacher she didn't relish her daughter having such an ungainly last name. The elder Pulvermacher retorted that the name had been good enough to get him into Buckingham Palace, where he was knighted.

Then Marutha changed her tune and began pushing the affair. She dropped Yaltah off at London's Grosvenor Hotel where she was supposed to meet Keith. Marutha gave her daughter a new coat and handbag, and then literally pushed her out of the car at the hotel as if she wouldn't need anything else since she would now being marrying a Pulvermacher.

When she didn't marry a Pulvermacher that made Marutha even angrier. Marutha gave Yaltah the silent treatment for weeks, and kept her away from her sister's wedding.

The failed attempts at matchmaking with my mother were not to be repeated with the more favored Yehudi and Hephzibah.

But matchmaking efforts for them began in March 1938, backstage after a concert at the Royal Albert Hall in London. Yehudi and Hephzibah were introduced to two redheaded Australian heirs -- Lindsay and Nola Nicholas.

There had been an earlier meeting between Lindsay and Nola and Moshe and Marutha in a hotel elevator, but it was apparently unplanned. They all knew each other only slightly. Still, Nola heard Marutha say, pointing at her, that she was the kind of woman she wanted Yehudi to marry.

Yehudi was smitten with the attractive redhead and they were married. Not too much later, Hephzibah married Lindsay in a wedding held at the elder Menuhins' Los Gatos abode.

Yaltah said that Marutha forbade her from attending that wedding. She was being punished for her failed first marriage to William Stix.

And, of course, Hephzibah was not to learn until later that her last communication with Fleg had been snatched from her by her mother. Indeed, she learned of Fleg's death only after she was safely married to Lindsay and living in Australia.

Some say that was what began the events that led to their eventual divorce.

In any event, Moshe and Marutha had had a kind of half-baked notion that when the children married they should return to the nest and live at Alma.

Like most utopian schemes, the idea never materialized. Moshe and Marutha pushed their children out of the nest early, but not entirely in earnest. Marutha so dominated Nola, Yehudi's first wife, that she destroyed the marriage.

It was over when Yehudi came home from a wartime concert tour and found Nola with another man -- a United States soldier.

Humphrey Burton says Yehudi tried to help Yaltah by smuggling her to Australia. Moshe raged at that, but what could he say? His son was now grown and a world famous figure. Various newspapers unkindly said Yaltah was looking for a husband -- which possibly was true. In any event, she again returned to her parents.

Then she tried to run away again. First, there was an ill-fated trip to the Juilliard School of Music, where she had almost no money and lived on cabbage soup while she studied piano with Carl Friedberg, who had been an associate of Brahms. She also had at least one nervous breakdown.

Friedberg knew who his very able student was immediately, but she thought she was fooling everyone by going under the pseudonym of Kate Davies. She borrowed the last name from Los Gatos friends and neighbors, the Davies family who owned the San Jose *Mercury News* before it was purchased by the Knight-Ridder chain.

Yaltah returned to Los Gatos, again feeling defeated. She kept developing crushes on various young men, including William Koshland, and writing poetry. She wrote a lot of poetry in 1939, almost always in French.

★

By the end of 1939, Yaltah was back with her parents in Los Gatos, and she began to write about dreams of long before, and flowers and spring and her lover who was alive in her heart.

She wrote about her melancholy, and wondered about her origins, and being the tree of her own destiny, about how everything was calm and far away.

She often sat on the beautiful Los Gatos hillsides at night and wrote about the song of the earth, the elongating tree shadows and the birds singing in the forest, and the cycle of destruction and creation that is the universe.

She sang about people seated in the shadows under the trees of the garden of the angels, and the tears, and the murmuring that invariably accompanies death.

She wrote about Debussy's "Girl With the Flaxen Hair," because its melodies drowned her grief. And to her lover, whoever he might be, she wrote about how his distant heart was full of fire, and how like a swallow flying into the sky at dawn he was. She wanted their love to be like a rose after a rain, arousing itself from its heavy sleep.

Alone with her parents, an increasingly desperate Yaltah wrote about finding a mate who would share the same heartbeat. She saw herself walking under night skies with him, peering into the heavens.

She loved to write poetry about inky night skies being swept away by luminous dawns, and lamented the passing of the stars, the divine light that dies at dawn.

Unfortunately, she also was developing asthma and hypothyroidism.

Marutha was about to force her into yet another sham marriage when she met my dad, which resulted in her leaving her unloving parents' abode forever. When they met, my

Moshe, trying to look dapper

father told my mother he was engaged to another woman whom he did not love.

★

My mom was desperate when she met my dad. She had started sneaking out and going to Army dances at nearby Fort Ord in Monterey. She soon ran away with one of the soldiers, my father, and married him in 1941.

Some years later, after the Rolfes had settled in Los Angeles to get away from the Menuhins, Marutha sent a gigolo to seduce Yaltah. Her hope was to break up the marriage.

Apparently the gigolo suddenly felt bad about the situation and confessed to Yaltah and Ben why he was there. Marutha's outrageous behavior would eventually take its toll on Yaltah's marriage.

CHAPTER ELEVEN

Joel Ryce

During the time she lived in Los Angeles, Yaltah was very much a musician's musician. She was a regular on the local concert stages, but her influence went beyond that. When a young musician wanted her endorsement for a Fulbright scholarship, her word was like gold. She was a regular at the "Evenings on the Roof" series where she played music she didn't particularly admire, but did so because she felt contemporary composers had to be encouraged. She also recommended cellist Gabor Rejto and violinist Eudice Shapiro for teaching positions at the University of Southern California's music school.

During her Los Angeles years Yaltah premiered works by Eric Ziesl, Mario Castelnuovo-Tedesco, George Antheil, Ernst Krenek and Walter Piston, among others.

After leaving her second husband, my father, Yaltah quickly gravitated to London in 1959 where she was reunited with her family by participating in a concert at the Bath Festival of which her brother had just become director.

She was so excited to see her brother at the first rehearsal she forgot to come in at the right place in the first movement of Mozart's Concerto for Two Pianos.

Later she mused to me that yes, she did come from an odd family. "We communicate better with music than words."

She said this at that Bath Festival appearance. There were to be more joint appearances with her brother and sister, and even some touring.

"We hadn't seen each other in six months. Yet when Yehudi walked in, we played as if we had been playing just yesterday," she said.

Six years later, on the occasion of Yehudi's fiftieth birthday at the Royal Festival Hall, Hephzibah, Yaltah and Yehudi's 14-year-old son Jeremy performed with the London Philharmonic Orchestra. The orchestra was conducted by Yehudi, and they played a rendition of Mozart's Concerto in F major for three pianos.

The 1960s were good years for Yaltah's piano playing, a culmination of a musical career that had begun in seriousness on the West Coast in the '50s. Despite playing some memorable concerts when she moved to London -- one for the Queen at Windsor Castle -- she tried to keep premiering works by contemporary composers.

For instance, she played a friend's avant garde piano music in London. It was aleatory, or "chance" music. The motifs would come from mobiles swinging in the wind, which blew in through the roof. She would improvise on musical phrases that were written on the mobiles. Such avant garde pretentiousness was not her style, but she still felt an obligation to participate.

Her talents were attracting notice. A review of one of her solo albums in the December 31, 1966 issue of the *Saturday Review*, put it well:

"Whatever else it may confer, having a famous name may often be as much a burden as an asset. In the case of Yaltah Menuhin, the burden has been sufficient for both shoulders. For, in addition to the shadow cast by her celebrated brother, she also has a piano-playing sister who, being earlier on the scene, absorbed the world's attention as 'another' first-class musician in the Menuhin family."

The review goes on to compliment her "lyric freshness" and "lightness and delicacy" as well as the kind of "comprehensive sense of structure" that does not try to inflate the music beyond its inherent dimensions. It pointed out that even *Grove's Dictionary of Music* didn't list Yaltah as a sister of Yehudi -- only Hephzibah.

About the same time as this review was published, Marutha wrote to her friend Esther Shak about how wonderful and great her son Yehudi was, but "the girls, again, are something else quite different -- but since they are by now our contemporaries we take no responsibilities and hope for the best.

"Yaltah's neglected sons are in an awful mess, but she is also old enough to know her own mind and evaluate the price of action," Marutha wrote.

By the 1970s Yaltah was under the strain of financially supporting her husband who had abandoned the piano, and eventually, as the years slipped away, she shifted away from music to help her third husband Joel's career as a Jungian therapist once his income eclipsed her own.

No one was happy about Yaltah's third marriage except the lovebirds themselves. Even Marutha sensed that Joel was using my mother. When Joel had a breakdown and landed in Zurich after a duo-piano world tour, Marutha described him as "a mental case in a hospital."

Hephzibah pleaded with me to get my mother to leave Joel. Hephzibah was asking no small favor. I am very much my mother's son, even in my complete rebellion from her. Yes, I admitted to Hephzibah, I was dubious about Joel. I knew he was a big economic drag on Yaltah. She was concertizing

Joel and Yaltah as a duo-piano team

to support him while he went through a mental breakdown, vowing never to touch the piano again.

Still, I told Hephzibah that I was not going to break up their marriage, that even if I wanted to, I would have no ability to do so. Later, Yehudi also asked me to try and break up my mom's marriage.

Between Yehudi's apparent complete adulation of his wife Diana and his mother Marutha, and Hephzibah's adoration of her own rather dubious second husband, Richard Hauser, Yaltah could have done worse. Joel was pompous, God knows, and was never likely to be remembered as a great pianist -- but he also was very intelligent and charming and not badly intentioned in a basic sort of way. He and Yaltah also seemed very much to love each other, even if in other people's eyes that love appeared misguided.

The inexplicable adoration of somewhat mismatched spouses was a Menuhin trait that began with the trio's parents -- and who knows how long before that? For if you go back that far, marriages were mostly arranged. Another trait of the Menuhins -- especially Marutha -- could be be the Byzantine reasons behind the curt dismissals. Once Marutha decided you were of no use to her, you were through.

Yaltah, after all, was born because of a diaphragm that didn't work, and Marutha, who died at one hundred and four years of age, never let her daughter stop knowing that. It was as if Marutha psychologically, not physically, was trying to do away with Yaltah because she was never perceived to be of any use.

When we were teenagers, my brother Robert and I used to get letters from Moshe. He would tell Robert not to become a scientist and me not to be a writer. He prescribed manual labor for us. Perhaps we should become ditch diggers or plumbers for that was more appropriate to our talents. Then he'd throw in a lecture about how noble common people are. My brother Robert, indicentally, became a physicist, and I have somehow made a living as a journalist and writer.

The Menuhin prodigies were very good at dissecting the

weaknesses in each other's marriages, if not their own.

I was sixteen when I met Joel in 1958 on my first trip to New York. My mother had just gotten together with him. I got quite nasty, unhappy perhaps that my mother was married to someone so much younger than my father. And he was only ten years older than I! My mom had left my dad to pursue her music, in part with my permission and even encouragement. But Joel wasn't what I had expected.

So I told them what I thought of their duo-piano work. Joel was a pounder, I said, like his roommate at Juilliard Van Cliburn had been, whereas my mother was incredibly sensitive to the music, portraying the mood and message of the composer with great precision.

★

It's a strong tendency all the Menuhins -- Yaltah included -- shared. They would rhapsodize excessively about their spouses.

I found it all too strange that Joel became a Jungian analyst after he had a mental breakdown and decided never to play another note. He did just that. He wouldn't even sit down at a piano -- and he was obviously uncomfortable even when Yaltah did so.

That was like torturing my mom. But for some reason she accepted it.

Still, although his death on March 31, 1998, devastated her, she began to flourish at the end of her life.

The following year Yehudi died.

Why Yaltah chose to fall and stay in love with Joel for thirty-eight years eludes me. How she could have loved a man so manipulative as Joel is open to conjecture.

He was, despite my mother's loyalty, certainly not a great musical talent. He definitely was not Yaltah's match.

The year before he married Yaltah, Harold C. Schoenberg in *The New York Times* had described Joel as a "facile technician," "a neat workman and an honest musician" who had a professional approach "but somehow, he did not have much to communicate."

When he hitched his star to a Menuhin, his publicist was quickly ordered to send out an announcement of the wedding to the press.

Joel was able, after he was securely married to a Menuhin, to write my brother and me in December of 1960, saying that he was speaking for himself and my mother, who was away on tour. Robby missed his mom and had asked to come live with them. Since I knew Joel, I was supposed to fully interpret the letter.

"We are very poor and will not take you here under any circumstances," Joel wrote. "As soon as this year's touring stops and we pay off our debts, we shall move into an even smaller place where, of course, there could be no place for you. The best possible answer to your life is to realize once and for all that your mother after years of unhappiness with the Rolfe men -- after their trouble-making, their discourtesy -- and if they did not follow the high example of their mother when they had the chance -- then for once and for all-- let it be clear that your mother no long feels any responsibility for anyone concerned -- when she remembers the way she was treated for years by all of you."

He went on to say that "it is very selfish of you now to even think of imposing on your mother's last chance to make a success of her life. You all came near to destroying her, but I and her family and our lawyers will see that none of you ever get near her again -- unless she wishes it for a brief period when and IF she can afford the time and money."

Joel's advice was that Robert should "be placed in the cheapest possible boarding school on the West Coast."

In a letter to his lawyer, telling him that he would not pay for Robby's support in a school, he said, "If Mr. (Ben) Rolfe thinks after maligning the Menuhins for years that he is now going to throw the product of his ruination, namely his own, on any Menuhin doorstep, we shall fight that without reservation."

It was odd how quickly Joel assumed the identity of the Menuhin family while at least two of the Menuhins were not particularly anxious to claim him.

Yehudi would help out sometimes because he could see that Yaltah had her hands full supporting Joel's career change with her concertizing, even as he was making it difficult for her to do so. But he felt toward Joel as Hephzibah did, negatively. The more Joel studied to become a Jungian therapist, the more he insisted practicing, let alone her career, be severely curtailed.

Joel, who began calling himself Joel Ryce-Menuhin for his psychological work, was mentor to a group of Jungian analysts in London and was chairman of the Analytical Psychology Club and edited its journal, *Harvest*, among many other activities.

He wrote a book about Jungian sandplay, of course, and a more curious book called *Naked and Erect: Male Sexuality and Feeling*.

Yaltah and Joel were a striking pair. I thought he was a bit insufferable and pompous, but he was tall, with rich red hair. He looked like a lion, and had what an admirer called "a rich and eloquent booming voice." It helped him as he pontificated on various subjects, mostly philosophy and psychology, which he did often.

As the years passed and I grew up, Joel and I became more amicable, and we talked at depth upon occasion. He was definitely a dualist, who believed in "the other world" of ideas and great art, beyond this mundane and material world.

He converted to Catholicism toward the end of his life.

His politics were abominably to the right.

I remember on one occasion in Zurich, the mysticism permeating the place and Joel's talk became almost real to me. On my shelf I still have a volume called *The Glory of the Rose* -- with watercolor illustrations by Lotte Gunthart. Gunthart presented the book to Joel and Yaltah in 1972 when Yaltah played Bach Preludes, and short pieces by Schubert and Chopin.

The rose is, of course, a Jungian archetype.

The idea of archetypes seemed all terribly vague to me, until Joel opened the Gunthart book to a picture of a rose.

"That is an archetype," he said.

I looked at it and suddenly I thought I understood what he was talking about. There in Zurich, surrounded by stone castles and beautiful gardens, the rose as a symbol of something universal began to make sense to me. He asked me to keep studying it. The more I did, the more intense the idea of the rose became.

Maybe that was what Orson Welles was referring to with the burning of the sled with a rose on it at the end of "Citizen Kane." Or maybe "Rosebud" as various wags have suggested, had more to do with Mrs. Hearst's frequent and sarcastic comments about the size of Mr. Hearst's manly tool ... naked and erect.

CHAPTER TWELVE
Willa's Centennial

It was during my first visit to London in 1972 that I saw the premiere of a documentary about Yehudi. I wore a borrowed tuxedo and rode with my mother in a Rolls Royce to the premiere.

In the film called "The Way of Light," my mother was shown talking about me, and there I was, sitting next to her in the theater, as she claimed onscreen that she didn't realize just how great a genius Yehudi had been until she had her first son. I took this to mean that I was quite ordinary -- and if anyone should give a person credit for being special, you'd think it would be one's mother. But that has rarely been the Menuhin way.

The next morning we had it out. "You love your brother as if he were a god, the Messiah," I shouted at her.

My mother did not deny the charge. "He is, after all, a genius." She showed me a book; on its cover was Schneur Zalman, an impressive-looking gentleman who, almost three centuries earlier, had been the Jewish equivalent of a great guru. He was my direct ancestor, my mother told me, and the founder of the Lubavitcher dynasty, a Jewish cult with considerable influence in Israel and in the American Jewish community. My first thought was, "Oh no, another Yehudi." The thought was flip but the moment was important. Now I knew why I had left home early and spent so many years escaping the influence of my family.

★

The 1972 trip had begun in Zurich where my mother was staying while Joel was undergoing treatment for his nervous breakdown. At that point I had not seen my mother in almost a decade. She and Joel had moved to London shortly after I last saw them in New York. My mother and I exchanged many letters, but I felt her letters were rather generic -- my mother was full of rather useless advice, I thought, and in my turn, I suppose, I complained too much.

Things got off to a rocky start in Zurich because of the hold over Yaltah by Violet S. de Laszlo, a Hoffman-LaRoche drug company heir, who was also the executor of the Jung estate and a financial backer of Dick Nixon and a supporter of the American side in the Vietnam War. I had spent the '60s battling just such people. Violet was Joel's analyst and mentor.

Violet's house had a cornucopia of fine liquors and spirits, and I imbibed many of them -- much to my mom's horror. We had a tremendous fight over my getting drunk and insulting their hostess -- I guess in retrospect I was being a brat. My mom had rarely seen me drunk before, and I guess I *wanted* to shock her.

Yaltah and Joel ended up driving from Zurich to London. I flew there, and stayed at my aunt Hephzibah's while awaiting their return.

★

I returned to London later that year with a contract to write my first book, *The Menuhins: A Family Odyssey*. Yaltah told me many things -- and for that matter so did Yehudi. Both

were interested in research on their Lubavitcher ancestors --
who had often been musical prodigies singing religious songs.
Yaltah spent hours telling me the family story, but I'm afraid
it did not help the cause of family unity. Her parents in Los
Gatos immediately *disowned* me because of it and Yaltah once
again became a non-person. Yehudi, who had also spent many
hours talking with me for the book and had liked it in earlier drafts, suddenly turned hostile -- primarily because I did
not praise his wife or his mother.

★

One day back in London Yaltah complained to me that
her agent wasn't getting her enough concerts. We talked a while
and I found out she had canceled about half of her concerts
because of Joel's obstructive behavior toward her practicing
and playing. After he gave up the piano, Joel had promised
Yaltah he would not stand in the way of her career, but he
inevitably did. Her concertizing was their only source of
income, yet he always complained whenever she practiced -
- it was too loud, he had a headache, etc.

Naive and unworldly as she was, Yaltah seemed really surprised when I explained that no agent would bother to get
her concerts if she canceled half of the bookings he got.
That was seemingly a revelation to her.

As it happened, she had just received a letter and was in
a quandary. She, along with Yehudi and Hephzibah, was invited to perform at the centennial of Willa's birth in Lincoln,
Nebraska, and then to talk about her in an important tele-
vised interview.

There was probably nothing more she would have wanted to do than accept. The subject was dear and familiar, and
the accommodations and fees were good. But Joel com-

plained he couldn't go with her because Nebraska was too close to his birthplace in Sterling, Illinois; yet he wouldn't let her go without him. I was furious with Joel and thought he was being completely irrational. I told Yaltah that if she didn't go I would disown her as a son.

As it happened, my mom went to Lincoln -- along with Yehudi and Hephzibah -- and played a very good concert. There was also a lively conversation among the three about Cather. The concert and interview were broadcast nationally on public television on several different occasions. Joel did not go with Yaltah to Lincoln, and instead went to Sterling where Yaltah later joined him.

That Lincoln appearance may have been Yaltah's last bid for freedom in her marriage with Joel. After that she submerged herself in Joel's career as a psychotherapist, cultivated her own hobby of doodling and painting on everything from baskets to coffee cans to masonite boards, and did her best to make Joel happy.

It may have been the hardest thing she ever did -- fighting Joel to let her go to Lincoln, where so many years before, Willa had gone to the University of Nebraska after leaving Red Cloud. It seemed almost as if my mother was making one last stand for herself before abruptly conceding everything to Joel.

It was not easy for her, at that point in their marriage, to insist on going to Lincoln, but she did.

There were two main components of the Centennial at Lincoln. One was the appearance of the Menuhins, on stage and in the interview, and the other was the publication of a collection of photographs called *Willa Cather: A Pictorial Memoir.*

As befits an observance on the centennial of her birth, the *Memoir* has little emphasis on Willa's European roots;

everything focused on her roots on the North American continent.

Their arrival in Lincoln must have brought this home to all three Menuhins, who had to fly more than 3,000 miles to get from London to the land of endless wheat fields.

Of the 192 illustrations in the *Memoir*, 82 were commissioned for the memoir. The rest were contributed by the Cather family, or Cather repositories, including the University of Nebraska, from which Cather had graduated in 1895. The text was by Bernice Slote, author and Cather scholar.

Presiding over the event as chairman of the Willa Cather Centennial Festival Committee was Robert Knoll, the university's principal Shakespeare authority.

But the memoir, as the lynchpin of the festivities, concentrated primarily on the land from where Nebraska's favorite daughter drew her inspiration.

The haunting images contrasting primeval prairie land and the aspiring cities like Lincoln and Chicago, were faithfully documented. Cather's journey to Pittsburgh and finally to New York are a testimony to another day and age, when New York was regarded as the center of the universe. The memoir also paid attention to Virginia, where Cather was born, and to New England, Canada and New Mexico, among other places.

Little mention was made of Europe, however, which was at odds with the way the children saw Cather. Although Cather was an intensely American writer, she owed a tremendous debt to Europe. The Menuhins, who first met "Aunt Willa" in Paris, must have been uncomfortably aware of that at the Centennial.

The University of Nebraska's Willa Cather Centennial Committee welcomed the three Menuhins to Kimball Recital Hall on December 7, 1973, a century after Willa was born.

The official release of the *Memoir* was ten days later.

Emanuel Wishnow conducted the university's orchestra, and Ron Hull, the master of ceremonies, welcomed the Menuhins to honor their childhood friend and teacher.

The sisters played the Mozart Concerto for Two Pianos in E flat major, which Mozart had played with his own sister, and after an interview, Yehudi played the Beethoven Violin Concerto in D major.

The dynamics of their relationship had not changed since childhood. It was Hephzibah who walked with a purposeful stride, who coaxed the conductor as well as her sister to take another bow.

When Knoll interviewed them afterwards, Hephzibah and Yaltah had a difference of opinion, not a major one, but indicative of the differences in their personalities.

Hephzibah recollected that they all spent much time at Willa's, and she enjoyed the fact there was no piano there. She thought it was wonderful to get away from work for a while. Yaltah was more reverential. She said she was always more at home in a place with a piano than without, but implied she would make an exception for Willa's home not having a piano, for instead it had Willa.

Hephzibah and Yehudi next exchanged differing views on Willa's feminism.

Hephzibah began by saying she hoped she was talking for everyone in making her next comments about Willa and feminism. Yaltah interjected to say the others would speak up if they disagreed.

When Hephzibah noted that Cather must have suffered greatly for her inherent women's liberation sympathies, Yehudi dissented.

"I always saw her as being permanently in exile as a woman,

as a spirit," Hephzibah said. Yehudi replied that Willa hadn't espoused a liberationist's viewpoint, because she served art, which was her muse. "The aesthetic in literature, in painting, was a moral code she served," he asserted rather pompously.

Hephzibah assailed him with the view that Yehudi was equating responsibility and freedom as somehow incompatible in women. She felt that Willa was in a perpetual state of tension between her love of tradition and her love of freedom from tradition.

Yehudi replied that Willa took everything from Greek and Latin and all the great literature of Europe. She had adored the Czechs and Germans, many of whom were Catholics.

Cather's affinity for Catholicism may have sprung from the fact that when she grew up in Red Cloud, the local Catholic Church had all the great music, while the Baptist Church she had been taken to as a child did not.

Cather believed that a novelist's duty is not to document, but to relate the truth and the essence of things by creating an intense work of art.

There was music in her words, even if she didn't have a piano in her apartment. To Willa, even the music sung by the birds was important. In *The Song of the Lark* she wrote, describing the conquest of the raw plains, that "There was a new song in that blue air which had never been sung before."

The lark's music was a perfect accompaniment for the immigrants -- the Czechs, the Swedes, the Germans and the Russians -- as they planted orchards, wheat and corn and vegetable gardens, and raised livestock.

What is sad is not to know what the conversation between Willa and the Menuhin children (especially Yaltah about *Lucy Gayheart*) might have been. During the interview in Lincoln, Hephzibah said that Willa often talked about events and people and especially the new people in the books she was writing.

Both Yehudi and Hephzibah could not resist noting that Willa Cather was never a "dry academic." As Knoll questioned them, Yaltah, who shared her sister's and brother's dislike of academia, was more diplomatic than her brother and sister, and did not use the loaded term "academic."

"She would be quite carried away with the passion of the language and the message of the play, and would share these emotions with us," Yehudi said.

Yaltah, proudly remembering the times that Willa took just her and not her sister or brother to a play or a museum, apologized for being "greedy."

"She never tried to look at details, but her absorption and concentration were so contagious, I suddenly found myself going through her experiences. I've often wished I could have known her as an adult, but then maybe she wouldn't have been quite so open. Maybe it was our youth that made it possible," Yaltah said.

Hephzibah noted that "there was no generation gap" with Willa, no matter how large the age difference.

Hephzibah and Yehudi also quibbled over Willa's attachment to the land. Yehudi said he had learned from the music of her prose never to separate himself from the earth, from the compost heap. But Hephzibah noted that Cather felt compelled to seek the world's great cities where one's values could be tested in the marketplace of ideas.

Yehudi granted -- and here he seemed to be speaking for all of them -- that Willa had influenced him much more than he had realized. He said he had seen this while preparing for this particular concert, as the memories and associations came flooding back.

Years later, when Hephzibah died, a Pittsburgh woman, Mrs. John A. Shaffer, sent Yaltah a book about Willa Cather's stay in that town. She sent a copy of the book and a photo she had taken of the McClung mansion at 1180 Murray Hill Avenue where Isabelle and Willa had lived.

Shaffer wrote that she had seen a lot of love between the sisters at the Lincoln concert, adding, "Somehow the time will go on and you will find the means to endure. You are the person you are because of your great spiritual strength."

Yaltah said Hephzibah's face glowed during her final days

CHAPTER THIRTEEN

Deaths

The years after the Willa Cather Centennial were not easy or good for Yaltah, even before Hephzibah's fatal illness.

Yaltah was the sole support of the household while Joel trained to be a Jungian analyst, yet she was having an increasingly difficult time playing on any of the three Steinways that were still there in the London flat. He constantly demanded quiet so he could study.

Yaltah could not stand to be away from him. That's why she canceled so many of her concerts -- concerts she usually got to by train.

"It's good to see some rain, to rock on this swift train, tomorrow by this time I'll be with you again," was a typical entry in her journal.

"Suddenly lonely, time weighs upon the crowded heart, but all my pain will fade. We are not long apart. Hope fills the stormy day until I see your face. We must often say sweet words of thanks and grace," she continued.

Sometimes she just pondered things, noting that each room has unseen eyes in which "we recognize a thousand moments gone, a thousand songs and ears, and the sunsets glowed each summer, the snow storms blurred the street lights."

Her dreams -- which she became more aware of as Joel

continued his studies into the esoterica of Jungian dreamscapes -- captured her. At the same time, music had a diminishing role in her life because Joel insisted on silence at home.

My mother was thinking a lot about "dreams of renewal and rebirth and change, of something emerging both volcanic and gentle, a lion of strength and a beautiful bird in the garden of peace.

"I try to interpret the mysteries there. They return every night, in so many shapes and surrounded by old roads with heavenly landscapes ... a new view of wide lands after dark winding canyons and dangerous jungles ... your love has watched over me and kept me serene in the midst of strange beasts."

As she thought about people in her life who had helped her keep protected, she wondered if perhaps "it was Willa who smiles or Edith who loved us or the array of spirits who are ever on guard when we are sorely tried or is it Trivia?"

Yaltah was rediscovering the primacy of the earth.

"We drove outside of London into sweet country lanes," she wrote one day. "The forests were mysterious with fog and rose gardens and tiny cottages. We forget in the noise of our markets and shops that everything comes from the soil, thanks to the water."

As Yaltah kept on with her concertizing, but became increasingly involved in Joel's Jungian world, she contemplated how, "when I was just a girl a large bouquet with daphnes was given to me in Sydney years ago. I never saw a flower more similar to the stars with such a haunting fragrance.

"I always loved the sound of rain while practicing the piano, the smell of gardens ... an open window ... it brings back various lands when I was young and played the piano in various lands in country homes, in Villa d'Avray, in California too."

When Hephzibah was diagnosed with throat cancer in the late '70s -- Yehudi thought that her demanding life as a social activist was the cause -- Yaltah's dreams got worse.

When the traditional doctors couldn't cure Hephzibah, Yehudi sent her to dubious practitioners, such as the German naturopath who said a diet of carrots would cure her.

Ying Sita, a genuine Burmese princess and family friend who visited with my cousin Kron Nicholas one time, sleeping on my floor, flatly insisted to me that Yehudi had prevented Hephzibah from getting the traditional cancer cures that might have saved her. The carrot diet was the example she singled out.

Whatever the answer, Hephzibah's unsuccessful battle with cancer was long and drawn out.

One night Yaltah dreamt of planted flowers in muddy earth where suddenly she saw a sunken grand piano, waterlogged and buried. Her feet trembled above the sacred relic and in this strange dream she saw five icons of pale transparent jade and Nola, Yehudi's first wife, dressed in green, the young sweet bride of 1938, so full of hope. Next Yaltah dreamed of summer rain and music and festivals and finally she saw a narrow dark coffin in a path covered with glass to look like emeralds.

On a trip to Wales for more concerts, Yaltah thought of her sister facing further chemotherapy -- probably she should have had such treatments earlier -- and wrote that "heavy days are ahead to be patiently faced."

She felt grateful for her concerts, even if the weight of her sister's illness was always upon her. One night on the way home from a concert she noted that "snow was predicted but stars came instead in a very cold night" during the "last icy moments before midnight."

She sat in a square watching "the quiet birds" circling "like golden arrows steadily moving" across a shining Jupiter, and "a strange solemn sigh of relief" that rose from "the earth to give thanks for the gift of music and love" and as they "followed their patterns we continued our paths in unified mystery."

It was getting harder and harder for Yaltah not to think constantly of her sister. At a concert in London two sisters who played in the orchestra helped her dress for a concert.

"The oldest is more peaceful; the other lost her husband. They are the oldest and the youngest of a family of five. The sadder one looks brighter; the lonely one serene."

She thought that "for sisters playing strings" it must "be a joy to work so close and care about each other. We too, my sister and myself, keep separate and yet in common."

One evening she described herself as too weary to remember the week's many events. "I lie in quietness awaiting life's renewal. Each note was lived, prepared and played; some were better, some were worse, meanwhile the world with its politics continues its mess. Personalities conflict, powers clash and chaos everywhere has many faces. I'm grateful for the flowers offered by the orchestra .. daffodils and irises ... azaleas and pinks each one perfect and so full of light. I must have played two dates here for it says with thanks from all ... Mozart always restores serenity."

By the beginning of 1980 Hephzibah's impending death was weighing increasingly on her dreams and thoughts.

"What is happening now which makes me so sad? I have practiced today but with little delight. I have just studied the notes and tried not to think of my terror inside. I can't now remember having laughed or enjoyed any part of this week. It is gray like the rain and hopelessly empty but if only she called with her silvery voice and reported some progress in her fight to get well, I would jump with new strength and dance down the street to the tube to her house and rejoice beyond limits."

The next day she went to where Hephzibah lived amidst the bustling Center for Human Rights and Responsibilities, on Ponsonby Place a few steps from the Thames.

"What a joy to drive up to the house where she lives and to see her dear face and sit down for a chat ... how you carry yourself so slender and frail like a shrinking new moon." When she heard Hephzibah's voice, she said, it made her "remember new meanings and life over old dreams."

But Hephzibah was not getting better.

Hephzibah believed in families based on affinity; you create your own family, in other words. During one of her stays in the hospital, when Yaltah went to visit her, she was so delighted she proclaimed that "the blood will tell."

Revolutionaries from South Africa or Ireland gravitated to Ponsonby Place. Hephzibah told me that in these countries, the Center would one day have to work to protect the rights of the vanquished -- the whites in South Africa, for example. Richard was a Viennese who survived a concentration camp and emerged with a vision to save the world. He once had his head beaten in by skinheads for trying to stop "Paki-bashing." Hephzibah's whole life was about changing the world.

Although she fought for social change, she did so with a sense of reverence for her ancestors. Mussia, one of Moshe's sisters, had been a big influence on Hephzibah. Mussia was a social worker at the turn of the century in Jerusalem, and Hephzibah was head of UNESCO's Women's Commission many decades later.

When Hephzibah had a little more than six months to live, Yaltah noted that her sister's voice had become "a whisper from afar, a powerful strain across the phone. I tried to guess her inner thoughts but all I sensed was infinite fatigue, a patient's struggle against herself."

After her sister died, in 1980, Yaltah proclaimed that she was tired of tears, of sobs, of choking. The weight of her grief had grown steadily as she saw her sister's face, her father's eyes, her distant friends, and felt the blurring tears starting again.

Then she asked God, "Please let me know that what is here is nothing like what is gone and that I must see."

After her sister's death, Yaltah kept performing but she did so less and less.

Marutha far outlived her elder daughter -- she was 104 years old when she died in November, 1996. They had never reconciled.

Yehudi once apologized to me for the way he and Hephzibah had sometimes treated my mother. Yet it was obvious that although Yaltah understood some of the dynamics that were involved, she still internalized feelings that she was not worthy of a career such as her brother and sister had had.

How much was that a factor in her abandonment of her piano during the last years with Joel? At first she couldn't play because he needed quiet to study. Later when he had patients, she had to be quiet too.

Later yet Joel got cancer, and he lingered until 1998. At the hospital, Yaltah slept on the floor to be beside him.

The following year Yehudi died. I returned to London in 1999 after a long absence. My mom declared it was up to her to keep the family going, but you could tell she really didn't have her heart in it. She was inconsolably grief-stricken by all the deaths.

After Joel succumbed, Yaltah transformed her flat into a shrine-cum-museum in his honor, and still tried to carry on his work. But in the end she was to die a pianist.

Yaltah was in constant psychic and ultimately physical pain and told friends that she thought she was going to die, so overwhelmed was she by Joel's death.

Several times she told me that she was ready to die. I told her that that surprised me, considering how alive she seemed. But I could also sense her underlying discouragement.

She still climbed the three stories to her flat in West Hampstead every day, took out the trash, and went to the market at the corner. Along the way, she stopped and talked with her many neighbors who wanted to tell her their troubles.

She knew everyone's life story. A walk up Canfield Gardens to the Finchley Road Station produced a portrait of London so vivid, it mirrored the truth in Samuel Johnson's remark that he who grows tired of London is tired of life. My mom was regarded by some as an eccentric, particularly in her distinctive blue and bejeweled bohemian garb.

Her encounters with Norman Lebrecht, the music critic for *The Daily Telegraph*, suggest how people sometimes used and misused her.

Lebrecht was the rabbi of a small temple -- a shul -- at the end of Canfield Gardens near the Finchley Road tube stop. Often by the time Yaltah got to the end of the block, she was tired, and she would sit down on a bench outside the temple to catch her breath.

On one occasion, Lebrecht came out and invited her inside to look over the shul. Partly because she appreciated a chance to rest, and also because she was, in fact, fascinated by all things religious -- she had once studied Kabala with a great teacher in Switzerland, which is normally forbidden for women -- she went inside.

Lebrecht managed to transform this in his obituary about her in *The Daily Telegraph,* saying that Yaltah had been "seeking solace in a tiny neighborhood synagogue, in the Jewish faith that her parents had rejected as archaic and cruel."

In fact, Yaltah no more turned into a synagogue-goer in the last years of her life than she had been before. For many years she maintained a personal shrine with Jewish, Christian and Buddhist symbols.

But the English do love their eccentrics, and that certainly includes a little presumably harmless hyperbole now and then.

Lebrecht fancied himself a friend of Yaltah, although his obituary was the most demeaning of all the obituaries that were written about her.

Another of her friends on Canfield Gardens was the playwright, poet and novelist Bernard Kops, who wrote about the mad fascist Ezra Pound. He also wrote about Anne Frank and Kenneth Patchen. Several Holocaust survivors also lived on Yaltah's street, and my mother knew every one of their stories.

A good friend and neighbor was Baroness Muriel Turner, an "old" Labor Party Peer in the House of Lords. Another of her neighbors was a widow forced to work as a domestic. Ronan Magill, a world class pianist, who is not yet famous, also lived close by.

Bunny Moses, in whose arms Yaltah was to die, was perhaps her most devoted companion, and she lived close by, as did Ivan Ezekiel, another devoted friend.

★

During the last three years of her life, I managed to visit Yaltah in London a number of times -- because I was aware she might not be long for this world. On one occasion in March 1999, shortly after returning from one of these visits, my brother awoke me with a 5 a.m. phone call to tell me Yehudi had died.

No one had expected it. He was only 82 and, after all, his mother had lived to 104. I felt the need to conclude the portion of my life in which Yehudi had been a major force with some kind of ceremony. When I heard that a memorial was planned for him in Westminster Abbey in June, I decided it would be the appropriate time to return to London. That was the second to the last time I saw my mother alive.

I remember my first visit to London after not having seen my mother for more than a decade. It was 1998, and Joel had died not long before.

As I got off the plane, there were articles in most of the newspapers about a controversy involving Yehudi.

I wrote about this in my book *Death and Redemption in London & L.A.* (deadendstreet.com). It seems Yehudi had just published a letter -- written in collaboration with Rostropovich, Perlman and others--in *The Times*, blasting the movie "Hilary and Jackie," a film about the cellist Jacqueline du Pré. I instinctively sided with the movie makers, probably in part because I'm a journalist. Truth is a valid occupation and avocation.

I had also experienced my uncle's wrath. His complaints about the movie struck me as the same sort of faulty reasoning he had used against my first book, *The Menuhins: A Family Odyssey.*

The next night my mom and I went to dinner at the home of one of London's top violinists, where we talked about the movie.

Yaltah had seen the movie at its premiere after which the director had spoken about why he made the movie. His own family situation was similar to that of du Pré, he said.

In the movie, du Pré moves in with her sister and ends up borrowing her husband, with serious consequences. The two sisters part bitterly, and neither sees the other until Jackie's multiple sclerosis intervenes -- and Hilary takes care of Jackie.

I would have expected Yaltah to agree with Yehudi, but in this case she did not. Instead, she said the movie was honest and well done. She said, however, that she might not want to read the book from which it was adapted (du Pré's sister and husband wrote *A Genius in the Family*). Yehudi "discovered" du Pré at the Bath festival.

Yaltah told us the director said he had been confronted by a similar situation in his own family. For this reason, the way he approached the work was authentic. So "Hilary and Jackie" met with my mother's approval. Besides, I thought, who was my mother to be upset by a little abnormal psychology? She grew up with it.

Some of the people at the dinner table had known du Pré personally, and that, of course, gave focus to the conversation.

As the movie about du Pré depicted, there's no doubt men and women, mothers and sons, fathers and daughters, brothers and sisters, are intimately involved in each others' lives in myriad mysterious ways.

★

One of my last memories of Yaltah occurred early one morning -- at 5 a.m. -- as Ivan Ezekiel, a next-door neighbor, drove us to the Hampstead train station. It was still dark and windy and biting cold. Instead of taking the Gatwick

Express, I was catching a local train to the airport.

As we said goodbye, my brand new white hat, that I had purchased for my trip to London, was blown down onto the station platform, where large, dirty pools were forming from the driving rain. I hoped it wasn't fate trying to tell me something, but just then the wind suddenly gusted. The hat spun past me and landed in one of those pools.

"Damn," I said, chasing after it.

I wasn't going to catch it. Another gust of wind blew it to the feet of a nearby Englishman by the edge of the platform. He was a businessman with a massive hat and an immaculate business suit. He grabbed for my hat and handed it to me ever so politely. I marveled that the hat wasn't dirtier. And I was glad it wasn't ruined.

Yaltah and Hephzibah spent a lot more time together in Hephzibah's final days

The train was due, and I had a lot of luggage to get onto the train. So I didn't have time to be effusively American in my thanks, but I'm sure my face showed my appreciation.

The one thing that did make me nervous was my mom's joining in the chase for my hat. She was a bit wobbly, anyway, and her running straight down into the rail corridor scared me terribly.

I envisioned her veering off the platform in front of an oncoming train.

My concern was needless. When I looked up at the dingy electric sign, we had seven minutes before the train was due. We ducked into a shabby, glass-enclosed passenger shelter where I could watch the clock ticking off the minutes. There, clutching my fugitive hat for security, I hugged my mother, and wondered if this would be the last time I would see her.

It wasn't.

CHAPTER FOURTEEN

Immortality

On one of my last trips to London to see my mother, I met a woman, an artist and a film documentarian, who got on the plane in Philadelphia. I quickly learned her name was Willa Woolston and she lived on a boat in London.

I asked her if she had heard of Willa Cather. I hadn't known anyone named Willa other than the novelist.

She told me that she had been named after Willa Cather by her mother, who died when she was only four years old. She never learned from her mother why she so loved Cather's writings. Willa told me she had read Cather, but only her novels about life on the plains -- which provided her no clue as to her mother's love of Cather's writing. I told her perhaps her mother loved Cather's poetry or her expatriate writing or her writing about true artists.

I told her my mother knew all about Willa, and perhaps she'd like to meet her.

Like her name, there was something willowy about Willa -- and wise. She had something of a reputation in England in documentary films and as a portrait painter.

When Willa went to visit my mother, she left with a stack of rare books that had been given Yaltah at the concert in Lincoln.

Photo by Sasha Rosen

Yaltah and Lionel

I saw Willa again on my next London trip. My daughter Hyla and I visited her on her boat on the Thames. While the rain fell softly on the roof of her boat on the canal, we drank wine, listened to jazz and looked at some of Willa's artwork, which was quite good.

Willa told me she now understood her mother's love of Willa Cather's work. She had decided it must have been the writings about artists and Europe that had moved her mother to name her daughter after the great writer.

★

I had talked to Yaltah by phone only three days before her death in 2001, and she sounded fine. We were making plans for my visit in a couple of months.

Instead, Jeremy, Yehudi's youngest son, called me one night at the office where I worked for a news wire service in the press room of Parker Center, the main police station in Los Angeles. He told me Yaltah had died.

He said that he thought her death, of a heart attack, might have been caused by the very strenuous program she had played the night before at a children's concert.

She regularly played at the Orwell Park School. On this occasion, she played preludes of Chopin and Debussy, then danced down the aisle with the kids behind her, full of abandon, life and glee.

Some who saw it said she was the most exuberant they had seen her in a long time. She died the next night in the arms of her loving neighbor, Bunny Moses.

Bunny became angry as she saw Yaltah suffer a heart attack. "You're not going to die," she said with death-defying fury.

By the time the ambulance got there, it was too late.

At the concert at Orwell Park she had played all the Chopin preludes, which Chopin wrote when he was in Majorca with his lover George Sand, and also played some preludes by Debussy, and followed up with "Clair de Lune" as an encore -- an appropriate selection considering she was "a great lover of stars at night," the school's headmaster Andrew Auster said.

English papers noted in their obituaries that Yaltah had been enjoying a renaissance when she died.

She had given a haunting and much applauded performance of the Mozart B-flat major Sonata at a memorial concert for Yehudi in November of 2000 in London. It was the same work that she had played with Yehudi in 1938. She played it with Nicola Benedetti, the fourteen-year-old violinist from the Yehudi Menuhin School who gave a moving rendition

Lionel with his daughter Hyla (on his left) and Yaltah (on the right) during one of his last visits

of Chausson's "Poeme" at a memorial for Yaltah put on by her good friend Rikki Gerardy in a small church on October 14, 2001. Yaltah had played with Benedetti on several occasions, and the young violinist felt close to her.

The concert, which also featured Yaltah's nephew Jeremy, began on a late winter afternoon, only a week after what would have been her eightieth birthday.

It was held in Highgate, London, where her brother had lived at 2 The Grove, just a stone's throw away from the church. The imposing house next door to Yehudi's had been where Coleridge wrote about Kublai Khan's Xanadu.

Despite all the familial and historical resonance in it, the place seemed but an empty stage as the audience disappeared into the Highgate night. The artist they had gathered to celebrate was no longer there to share the joys -- and sorrows -- of music.

My mother's was a story full of frustrations, rejections, and timing mishaps. Being a Menuhin handicapped her but it also gave her tremendous advantages.

Baroness Muriel Turner and Lionel Rolfe at the memorial concert for Yaltah Menuhin, October, 2001, in Highgate, London -- Lorene Pike

By June of 2001 when she died, Yaltah was embarking on a flowering, a renaissance, after a long period of mourning. Her tale was truly like that of Cinderella. She had at last become the artist she was meant to be. She was playing more and more concerts, and was in a very real sense continuing the Menuhin tradition -- and fulfilling the dream that Willa Cather inspired in her.

It was a long time coming, the closure of this life Willa Cather in great part wrote. The best may have been toward the end, the tale in which Yaltah transformed herself from a Lucy to a Thea. It was a long time comging, but in the end Yaltah fulfilled the destiny Aunt Willa had written for her.

Yaltah, two years after Aunt Willa died

The three Menuhins

Set in Bembo with Ribbon Bold headlines. Three thousand copies were printed on acid-free 60-pound paper at McNaughton and Gunn lithographers, Saline, Michigan. Typography and book design by Ken Boor of The LA Type.